visual faith

Engaging Culture

WILLIAM A. DYRNESS
AND ROBERT K. JOHNSTON,
SERIES EDITORS

The Engaging Culture series is designed to help Christians respond with theological discernment to our contemporary culture. Each volume explores particular cultural expressions, seeking to discover God's presence in the world and to involve readers in sympathetic dialogue and active discipleship. These books encourage neither an uninformed rejection nor an uncritical embrace of culture, but active engagement informed by theological reflection.

visual faith

art, theology, and worship in dialogue

william a. dyrness

Baker Academic

A Division of Baker Book House Co
Grand Rapids, Michigan 49516

Published by Baker Academic
a division of Baker Book House Company
P.O. Box 6287, Grand Rapids, MI 49516-6287

Printed in the United States of America

Library of Congress Cataloging-in-Publication Data

Dyrness, William A.
    Visual faith : art, theology, and worship in dialogue / William A. Dyrness.
        p.   cm.
    Includes bibliographical references (p.) and index.
    ISBN 0-8010-2297-5 (paper)
    1. Art—Religious aspects—Christianity. I. Title.
BR115.A8D97 2001
246170—dc21   2001037487

For current information about all releases from Baker Academic, visit our web site:
www.bakerbooks.com/academic

contents

illustrations

Figures

Plates (following page 96)

preface

This book aims to extend and enrich a Christian conversation on the visual arts. As a conversation with a somewhat spotty history, however, there are historical, biblical, and theological issues that need sorting out. Since this book is written by a theologian, these issues take prominence over questions of art history or current challenges in the practice of visual arts—though comments are offered on these fields where they are relevant. As the subtitle indicates, it is also my purpose to bring questions of visual arts and theology into dialogue with worship. I do this for two reasons. First, it has become my conviction that the practice of worship provides the most appropriate setting for a fresh appraisal and even a renewal in the arts. Worship calls us to respond actively and intentionally to God's glory as it is revealed in Jesus Christ and empowered by the Holy Spirit. Contrary to what our tradition may have taught us, therefore, I believe that making beautiful forms is theologically connected to our call both to listen and respond to God in prayer, praise, and sacrament. I provide historical and biblical reasons for this claim. Second, the conversation about worship is not only appropriate today, it is more urgent than ever before. The current revival of worship is forcing Christians to rethink the shape and patterns of our corporate life before God. It may also provide a unique opportunity to recover our Christian heritage of the visual arts—as well as of other art forms.

The goal I have set for this book is to provide, within the limits of my abilities, a brief survey and evaluation of the current discussion about these issues, and then to sketch out some possible directions for the future. Though it is written from the perspective of an evangelical Protestant, and therefore addresses issues unique to that community, it seeks to connect with the broader Christian conversation on the arts. When referring to visual arts, I am working with the following definition: The visual arts embrace any visual object or production that is a personal and intentional expression of an artist who is usually, though not always, professionally trained and employed, either working alone or in collaboration with other artists, without direct reference to commercial value. The work of making and enjoying fine art, then, is a "highly specialized activity requiring considerable learning and patient application from its practitioners and primary audience."[1] The focus here will be largely on what is usually considered fine art—painting and sculpture—and contemporary art forms descended from these—installations and performance art. Though I am particularly alert to more popular forms of art and their use in worship and the wider culture, these are always discussed in relation to the fine arts. There is obviously no timeless character to any such definition, for every definition is embedded in a particular setting (and indeed this definition itself is currently under challenge, as we will see), but we must start where we are. For this reason, at every point I seek to put the discussion of visual art in its larger cultural context. Indeed, I am anxious to see the way the visual captures and focuses values found in the broader culture. For this reason, too, I make occasional reference to music or literature as places where cultural values similarly come to expression.

There are obviously many ways in which these questions could be approached. One might, for example, speak of the way Christian use of the arts parallels or contrasts with other religious traditions and their use of art; one might speak not of Christian artists but of the Christian public and ask how they might want to interact with the art world, whether Christian or non-Christian; one might spend more time focusing on the secular art world, discussing ways in which God is also present and at work there. These questions, though important, for the most part are outside the scope of this book. Here I address primarily Christians who have some involvement (whether formally or informally) in art. While I am not interested solely in "Christian art," that is, art made with a clear Christian subject or for religious purposes, I do place a major emphasis on art made by Christians, for these artists face particularly daunting challenges as they seek to work to the glory of God.

Since it deals with such enormous (and highly charged) questions, a book such as this is never finished. It is more appropriate to say that at a certain point it is simply abandoned. And if it were not for help from some friends, the results would have been even more meager than they are. Robert K. Johnston (my coeditor in this series) and Jeremy Begbie read the entire manuscript and made helpful comments, though they should not be held accountable for the final product. My editor at Baker, Robert Hosack, has been a particularly enthusiastic supporter of the work, and it would never have been finished without the faithful support of our faculty assistant, Beth Webb, and my student assistant, Diane Chen. Larger academic debts are acknowledged in the endnotes, but a more personal debt is owed to my students over the years whose eager questions always made me think harder about the intersection of faith and art. I dedicate this book to the students in my theology and art classes who, more often than not, took the material not only into their hearts and minds but into their lives and churches. They represent the hopeful future, for the sake of which this book is written.

introduction

The Uneasy Relationship between Art and Faith

We begin our conversation with the recognition that, in recent history at least, art and the Christian church have not been on good terms. In fact, when considering Protestant churches in general, while there are exceptions, it is fair to say that this tradition has had a troublesome history with the visual arts.

Two examples may stand as representative of our current situation. Recently, a Christian artist told me about an experience with his mainline Protestant church. He has been an active member of his church for some time. Not long ago in an effort to express his appreciation for his community of faith, he gave what for him was the best gift he could give: He donated one of his paintings. He told me how the nonplussed church leadership expressed their appreciation as best they could, but it soon became clear that they did not know how to make use of the gift or, indeed, of the talent it represented. For a time the painting hung in the church hall, and then it disappeared altogether. The experience left my artist friend surprised and disappointed. This episode, which unfortunately is not an isolated incident, is telling not only of the missed opportunity it expresses but also of the habit of mind it illustrates.

Or consider this example. Recently, I visited the Boston Museum of Fine Arts, which contains one of the best collections of early American art in the world. The period of American history emphasized by the collection—from the founding of the country to the mid-nineteenth century—surely encompasses some of the important religious periods of American history. But the visual art that remains from this period contains little reference to the Christian faith, was not made particularly to aid Christian worship, and does not even illustrate a particular Christian belief. Many of the artists were more than likely Christian, and perhaps their faith influenced their work in many subtle ways. But before the nineteenth century at least, they chose not to make any explicit reference to their faith. The reasons for this are certainly complex—relating to the role

11

of the artist in the community, patronage, and religious attitudes toward the arts in general—but clearly some important issues relating to Christianity and the visual arts were also involved.

These two illustrations underline the complexity of the issues that are addressed in this book. On the one hand, art with a clearly Christian intent is rare in the Protestant tradition—though, as we will see, important allowance must be made to what we mean by "clearly Christian intent." The Protestant tradition, for various reasons, has developed a complex and sometimes difficult relationship with the visual arts. On the other hand, this does not mean that there were and are no talented Christian, particularly Protestant, artists. Both my friend and the artists whose work is displayed in the Boston Museum illustrate this point. Their connection with the church, and even more particularly with worship, however, has not always been mutually enriching.

But even this may be an understatement. Not only is the environment of Protestant churches not conducive to producing Christian art, but it turns out that it may actually impede the development of artistic imagination. At least that is what Andrew Greeley argues in a recent book. Comparing a sample of Catholic and Protestant churchgoers, he found that frequency of church attendance correlates dramatically with fine arts involvement among Catholics, but it does not correlate significantly with Protestants.[1] But that is not all. Greeley developed what he called a "grace scale" to measure people's sensitivity to religious imagery. Respondents were asked to describe their view of God as mother versus father, lover versus judge, spouse versus master, friend versus king. For Catholics, again there was a high positive correlation between a high score on the grace scale (that is, a preference for the first item of these pairs) and fine arts involvement. For Protestants, the more frequently they went to church, the lower their score on the grace scale. If Greeley is correct, this finding suggests that there is something about attendance at church that may actually discourage the artistic imagination.

In this book, then, I explore the relationship between art and faith in general, but I go farther and inquire into the relationship between the visual arts and worship in particular. This involves spending some time thinking about the historical antecedents to the current situation. Obviously, Protestants and Catholics share an important historical legacy. Somewhere along the line, however, it appears that Protestants lost touch with a vital part of their heritage, for during many periods before the Reformation, the church held a virtual monopoly on the best art (and also incidentally on the best music and literature). I examine these periods of Christian history in chapters 1 and 2 and attempt to provide reasons for the abandonment of the visual arts by many Christians. This historical exploration raises an important series of questions: Did the Reformation church have good biblical and theological reasons for giving up on the visual arts? If not, what was the real motivation behind their attitudes? And what, if anything, can be (or is being) done to repair this breach?

These questions form the heart of this book. Focusing in particular on the Protestant tradition, and even more particularly on the Reformed part of that tradition, I consider the historical, cultural, and even theological factors behind the apparent estrangement that exists between Protestants and the visual arts. I hope to reveal the factors that led Christians to become involved in the visual (and other) arts in significant ways, both before and after the Reformation. But I also want to inquire into reasons why, later in the tradition, this involvement stopped, so to speak, at the door of the church. No single book, indeed, not even a single generation of Christians, can hope to answer these questions completely, but I hope at least to clear the ground so that we might see where these answers may be found.

Contemporary Revival of Christian Involvement in the Visual Arts

Protestant Christians in some ways never left the arena of the arts, but after the Reformation the arts were no longer welcomed into the church. For their part church leaders and architects worked with priorities that pointedly excluded visual artists. The spaces made for worship were not friendly to elaborate visual elements, for they were seen as distractions from true worship, which always focused on the preached Word. Creative people, then, understandably turned their imaginative energies in other directions—literature and music became special foci for Protestant creativity.

But the discussion should not end at this historical level, for things are clearly changing at the turn of the new millennium. In fact, one might go so far as to speak of a revival of Christian interest in the visual arts. Christian art groups and magazines have proliferated in the last generation. Seminars and conferences on topics related to the arts and worship are being offered more frequently—often across denominational lines. Meanwhile, much work currently being done by Christian artists is of a high quality, even as this is measured by the artistic establishment. These artists show their work in fine galleries and teach in prestigious art programs. Art departments at Christian colleges are improving, and there is even talk of a MFA designed for Christian artists. (See the bibliography for information about some of these resources.)

In the larger world of popular culture, the Christian presence is receiving new attention. In many ways, Christians have often embraced popular culture. One thinks of revival choruses and tracts and the role of music in the black church. But in the late twentieth century, Christians became more intentional about their engagement with popular culture. In the '70s, the Jesus People movement influenced the rise of what is now known as Christian gospel, with its own Grammy-award category and an enormous following—even among secular music enthusiasts. At the end of the century, TV programs and movies increasingly featured Christian themes.

In churches, especially fast-growing charismatic and mega churches, visual and dramatic arts are becoming a standard part of worship. Special effects, dramatic skits, movie clips, slides of artwork, to say nothing of worship bands, are common in "contemporary" worship services. While some may doubt whether these works and compositions will stand the test of time, or whether they are contributing to truly biblical worship, clearly there is creative energy—and excitement—here.

In an important sense, these developments focus even more clearly the problem addressed in this book, for these enthusiasts are working with serious handicaps. First, they have had to overcome centuries of neglect in regard to art that reaches back to the Reformation. This neglect came to a spectacular focus during the latter years of the nineteenth century and the early years of the twentieth century, when evangelical Christians increasingly concentrated their spiritual energies on the inner life. In the early part of the twentieth century, due to the growing influence of liberalism in churches (and culture in general), many of the most serious Christians withdrew altogether from involvement in the broader culture. As a result, during this time the arts (including popular art forms such as movies) developed with little influence from Christians.

In the last twenty-five years, however, evangelical Christians have jumped into the cultural arena with both feet. They have become involved in almost every conceivable area of culture in an unprecedented way. In the case of the arts, it is significant to note that it is precisely in the area of worship—within the walls of the church—that this revival is taking place. As a result, vast quantities of creativity have been placed at the service of the church and its mission.

At this point, however, two further problems have intervened. First, musicians and artists have had to come to terms with the artistic and commercial establishment that supports the arts on the one hand, and with the Christian community (or subculture) on the other. With respect to the first, Christian artists wonder if their "spiritual" content will be accepted in the artistic establishment. With respect to the Christian community, there is continuing worry that artists will oversimplify their message in the interest of selling their work or of placing it in "secular" galleries. (This parallels the way Christian music groups are accused of "toning down" their lyrics to be more commercially viable.) I describe below some of the mutual suspicions that impede these relationships.

Second, because of the historical relationship between Christianity and the arts, alluded to above, the involvement of Christian artists in the church is necessarily fraught with tensions. These artists are not working with a clear theological or artistic consensus, a coherent cultural strategy, or broad-based community support. Therefore, they are necessarily placed in a situation of negotiation and compromise. Creatively, artists are forced to make do with bits and pieces—retrieved from their long-forgotten Christian heritage or from other

Christian traditions, or borrowed from their secular context. The results, one must conclude, are uneven at best. But it is shortsighted to leave things here. With reference to the arts, this is a critical period in the history of the church. While the challenges are great, the opportunities have never been greater.

Confusion (and Excitement) in the Visual Arts

This revival in Christian involvement in the arts in some ways parallels an equally important upheaval in the secular art world. While there is still a fair amount of public interest and support for the arts, broadly conceived, there is a great deal of confusion about the status and future of what has traditionally been known as the visual arts—painting, sculpture, and graphic art. Laurie Fendrich, a professor of art, recently put the current situation in these terms: "Before modernism, painting was the noise in the culture, because it attracted attention. Now, the culture is the noise, and painting . . . attracts little attention, either in the culture at large or in the art world."[2] Thomas McEvilley similarly noted that painting has petered out for forty years or so. "Our culture's long obsession with this art form as its channel to reality has been loosening . . . in favor of the conceptual object."[3]

This change resulted in part from technological developments, such as the invention of photography and later the moving image. These advances democratized both the making and, even more, the consumption of art products. But beyond this, the current upheaval in the arts resulted from a sea change in our culture known as postmodernism, a name given to the contemporary situation of cultural and religious pluralism. Our culture no longer shares deep underlying values that can find expression in widely appreciated works of art and communal projects of architecture. Rather, each of the various ethnic, lifestyle, and generational subcultures has its own particular art values and pursuits.

Further, the objects that focus the attention of the public today are no longer great works of art and architecture at all. Rather, attention focuses these days on popular culture—especially that which focuses on movies, television, MTV, and now the Internet. The rise of these media has had a great influence on the production of "art"—those products created by (usually professional) artists to make a personal statement. Some have sought to explore the potential of these media for production of new forms of visual art. This has led to a generation of video artists, such as Bill Viola and Nam June Paik, who have regular exhibitions in major American (and European) museums. These artists share one thing in common: They have been raised on a steady diet of TV and videos. They share with their generation a propensity toward the visual, especially moving images, that is both reflected in and influenced by popular media. Their art celebrates this burgeoning and bewildering proliferation of images and sounds that has become the normal environment of the early twenty-first century.

Many artists, of course, deplore these artistic developments. They want to resist the influence of popular culture and insist on the importance of more traditional forms of "fine art." Even abstract art, which used to be considered cutting edge, is now sometimes dismissed as traditional and static. But many would support Professor Fendrich's argument that abstract forms are important because they "defy translation into data, information, entertainment, rational image or any kind of narrative. [They] present an ineffable balance of sensation, experience, and knowledge."[4] Thomas Crow sees the challenge as primarily between artists intent on expressing their own sensitivities in these new forms, and those who formerly worked within a discipline with standards and practices internal to itself. Many celebrate street fashion, film, and other forms of "visual culture," he notes, without realizing that these too require new and complex critical competencies. There may well be masterpieces there too![5]

Ironically, it is possible that these new media, often anathema to traditional art lovers, will stimulate a revival of more traditional forms of art and communication. Just as Amazon.com has given traditional books—thought by many to be an outdated medium—a new visibility, on-line art sales may stimulate more traditional art forms. Large auction sites, such as eBay and the Sotheby/Amazon partnership, and the growing practice of artists selling directly to the public through their own web sites seem to be stimulating the sale of traditional works of art, which after all still look better on the living room wall than does a five-minute video! Internet sites that display works of art, even on-line video clips, from museums are making traditional (and contemporary) art available to anyone with a computer and a modem. What will come of this and what the art forms of the future will look like is still unclear. But the level of energy and creativity that surrounds these new ventures in art is clearly remarkable.

The changes in art production are matched by an equally important change in the institutions that promoted (some would say "constructed") modern art in the twentieth century. A few important museums and galleries, primarily in New York, played an important role in creating what Nicholas Wolterstorff has called the institution of high art—art that is visited and enjoyed only in museums or galleries and is made only for the purpose of aesthetic enjoyment. It is evident that the monopoly of the institution of high art is being threatened. Art making is no longer the unique province of artists making products for museums and concert halls, nor is art made only for the purposes of aesthetic contemplation.[6] In the glory days of modern art, during the middle years of the twentieth century, only the art noticed by significant gallery owners or by a small group of museum curators was able to bring the artist (and the dealer) fame and fortune. The gatekeepers of the art world were a small group who zealously guarded its power. As a result, it was not difficult to keep track of important developments in this world. In New York in 1960, for example, there were only roughly a dozen important galleries. One could visit them in an afternoon. By 1987 that number had risen to more than four hundred![7] Whether these hundreds of galleries, and even the major museums of that city, were all showing something of worth is doubtful. But clearly the art monopoly was disintegrating.

A major reason for this critical shift lies in the growing presence and influence—one is tempted to say the triumph—of popular culture and its ever present visual media. The avant garde, or what might be called the cutting edge of the arts, is no longer the purview of painters or sculptors, nor of the galleries and museums that show their work. It has been taken over (at least partially) by the producers of TV commercials, the rock stars and their music videos, and even by fashion designers. This means that, for better or worse, the dominant artistic influences in the culture today are to be found among the popular arts, not among what used to be called high art.

This may explain why today everyone even remotely associated with art or design is called an artist. In a conversation I had recently with a fellow Californian, he mentioned that he was an artist. I asked what kind of art he made. "Oh," he said, "I design eyewear." Even glasses have been brought into the domain of art, and their designers are artists!

A major reason for these developments has to do with patronage, that is, who puts up the money for art and therefore decides what kind of art is produced. During the Middle Ages and the Reformation the patrons of the arts were the church (cardinals and popes) and wealthy families (such as the Medicis in Florence). More recently their place was taken in Europe by governments and public agencies, and in America by wealthy collectors. Now these patrons have been supplanted by giant commercial interests—the music, fashion, and advertising industries. Today these industries support various artistic products, which are made to serve the overriding commercial goals of the patron. This shift in patronage surely will have important consequences. Previously, wealthy art collectors were able to influence public perceptions of art, especially as they developed public art collections in America. Now giant commercial interests are playing an increasingly visible role in popular culture and in the making of art more generally. This is becoming true in Europe as well.

These developments present a range of challenges and opportunities for Christians. On the one hand, given that Christians have not until recently involved themselves in popular culture, we should not be surprised that these arts often express values that are at odds with a Christian worldview. In fact, it is tempting to say that until Christians and the church get serious about supporting the arts, they ought to temper their criticism about the kind of art that is produced. Meanwhile, if they are serious about their involvement in culture, they should take seriously their role as patrons of the arts. On the other hand, this commercial involvement is not necessarily the disaster for the arts that it is often made out to be. Simply because a commercial interest puts up the money for a project does not mean that the artist cannot make a work of art that is worthy and in some way contributes to human flourishing. Art today often involves a collaboration among several players who represent various skills and interests. Such a situation should be seen as an opportunity and not necessarily an obstacle for the Christian observer.

Note that high art, the kind featured in large public museums, has not disappeared. While it may not have the prominence and influence it once possessed, it still represents an extremely important sector of the art world. One way of looking at this situation is to see that while the worlds of high and popular culture used to have clear, defined boundaries, these boundaries are being eroded. Clearly, the two cultures still occupy separate worlds, but these worlds overlap and interact at many points.

A cynical way of describing the situation is to say that the world of high art is in the process of being co-opted by popular culture. Indeed, when it is successful, high culture often becomes a part of popular culture. Consider, for example, the increasing prominence of so-called blockbuster shows of major artists. In 1999, more than 800,000 people visited the Los Angeles County Museum's "van Gogh's van Goghs," and 316,000 went to see "Picasso: Painter and Sculptor in Clay" at the Metropolitan Museum in New York. As with all-night rock concerts or super sales, hours for such shows are often extended (the van Gogh exhibit and the Boston Fine Arts Museum's John Singer Sargent exhibit were open twenty-four hours a day toward the end of the show).[8] Art is becoming a cultural event, not unlike the rock or film festival. The artist, as a result, becomes a cultural icon, gracing T-shirts and coffee mugs.

Some museum officials are clearly troubled by this trend. Brent R. Benjamin of the St. Louis Art Museum expressed his concern this way:

> This is a real concern to museums because the number of people who come through the door is only one measure of success. As important are the experiences people have inside. If you're chasing numbers alone, you have a narrow range of topics to choose from. The greatest challenge for museums is to build an audience for exhibitions that are not Impressionism or antiquities.[9]

That is, how does one keep the art that is intended to challenge people's perceptions from becoming captive to popular taste and current fashions?

Again one should not oversimplify a complex situation. One might be cynical about the marketing of Beethoven's "Greatest Hits" or van Gogh's "Starry Night" T-shirts, but these strategies are making available to a broader audience a larger repertoire of cultural products than any previous generation had at its disposal. When someone sees a painting of van Gogh, whatever the context or motivation for the visit, the potential exists that the encounter with a highly nuanced and complex work of art can deepen that person's understanding of the world.

We will have occasion later to question the unique status a work of fine art has been assigned in the postmodern period. But even if we do not believe that artists are gifted with a special vision of reality, we can still insist that fine art—that is, self-consciously creative visual work that displays a thoughtful awareness of its cultural and historical context—has a critical role to play in the larger culture.[10] A carefully wrought and intelligent object or painting, when it is patiently observed, opens up windows on the human situation in a way that other cultural products cannot. And this can be just as true of work created by non-Christians as that done by Christians.

Notwithstanding the unique role of the fine arts, it remains true that most people's aesthetic preferences are exercised in the formation and enjoyment of popular culture. Paul Willis, in fact, has argued that in an important sense the real creativity today is at the street level. He argues that consumers are not simply victims of advertising but are making choices that clearly express their own symbolic creativity—witness the change in advertising strategies from age groups to lifestyle categories, which has changed completely the way marketers think about their audience. Clearly, there is much creativity at the level of consumers of popular culture, and it is expressed in the way people decorate their homes, arrange the table for guests, or even in the clothes they wear. The best way forward then, Willis argues, is for purveyors of high culture to work in closer partnership with popular culture and thus make available a broader range of symbolic materials for creative appropriation.[11] These issues of popular taste and art as a commodity raise fundamental questions, not only about the nature of art but also its function in our postmodern culture, to which I will return frequently in this study.

We have noted that the cultural products of large commercial enterprises have played an important but ambiguous role in our culture. Their influence has certainly not been entirely negative. Indeed, in many ways these companies have set themselves a high artistic standard. Take, for instance, the Grammy-award celebration, or even the latest Superbowl-inspired TV spot, both of which reveal the very latest in visual effects, clever editing, and mixing. Note that in these arts, and in popular culture generally, visual effects are always accompanied by words and music. This dazzling display, however, can serve to hide what is at stake in these developments. Anyone with experience in these large industries soon discovers that beneath the glitter deeply spiritual battles are being fought. Images of home and family, of reconciliation and friendship compete with those of violence, lust, and revenge. Indeed, many power brokers within these industries possess a violent hatred for anything overtly religious let alone particularly Christian. Many Christian artists could tell stories of blatant discrimination that, if practiced against an ethnic minority, would quite properly be subject to litigation.

But it would also be foolish to suppose that these battles are always lost, or that Christians should not be involved, for we are confident in God's rule, believing that nothing is completely outside his authority. Not even moguls can predict what will capture the hearts and souls of people. Recall, for example, the impact of the blues, the Beatles, or more recently rap music. Consider also the recent popularity of outsider and folk art. These remind us that "the impetus of stylistic creativity [comes] from below."[12] And this creativity is frequently accompanied by deep spiritual longings. New movements can provide glimmers of God's presence in culture and models that Christians can utilize. Moreover, the influence of the World Wide Web on culture and the visual arts has created an interaction that no commercial interests can control completely. Here popular culture may take on a more genuinely democratic character, though the shape and impact of this remains to be seen.

For purposes of this discussion, I want to emphasize how powerful and pervasive are the visual dimensions of contemporary popular culture. In fact, a typical criticism of contemporary culture is that images have come to count for more than words.[13] One need only consider the power of TV advertisements (even with the sound off!) or of the dazzling visual effects seen on giant movie screens or in billboard graphics. The power and pervasiveness of these images is a complex issue that Christians clearly need to address, and one that should not be oversimplified. But fears about such things can easily be overstated. Christians, after all, believe humans are created in the image and likeness of God and that creation was lovingly and artfully shaped by the hand of God. Humans, therefore, even in their fallen condition, are capable of making worthy art. God as creator and sustainer still holds the world in his hands. Christ, moreover, rules culture as the risen and ascended Lord. These facts alone should stimulate Christians to be concerned with the visual dimension of life and the power of images that surround them. And of all the images that matter, those that serve as the personal expression of artists, whether Christian or not, should concern us most deeply.

In addition to the theological grounding for the importance of the image (something explored in chapter 4), there is another important reason to pay attention to the visual arts. The contemporary generation has been raised and nourished by images; it has an inescapably visual imagination. Regardless of whether one considers this good or bad, for this generation, aesthetics counts more than epistemology. Actually, this is a theme that has deep roots in the Christian tradition. As St. Augustine put it, what you enjoy (love!) is more important than what you know! Critiquing contemporary culture has been a favorite pastime for Christians since the Reformation. It is too easy to forget that our contemporaries, whatever their weaknesses, are human and still bear the image of God, and since they indwell an ordered world that God made, they still have an intuition of truth and a moral sense (whether they admit these things or not). But the way into these sectors of their lives is, more often than not, through aesthetics—art, drama, and music. These dimensions of life provide the key to unlocking the heart of the generation reaching adulthood—the aesthetic life and pursuit of the inner world comprise the emerging disposition of this era.[14]

This means that we must think not only about words and truth, however congenial this discourse may feel to those of us raised within the walls of traditional churches. It is true that the Protestant imagination has been nourished uniquely by the spoken and written Word, and therefore, we tend to think that everyone must be spiritually and morally nourished in the way that we (and our forebears) have been. Surely these verbal means are of critical importance. But our children and their friends have been raised in a different world; they are often uninterested in our traditional word-centered media. Instead, they are looking for a new imaginative vision of life and reality, one they can see and feel, as well as understand. And their attention span for sermons and lectures is notoriously short! We, of course, believe that the Bible and the Christian tradition are primary resources for a recovery of vision. But we must listen carefully to this generation and reread Scripture in the light of their dreams and fears. Then perhaps we will present the gospel and plan our worship in ways that respond to their quest and reintegrate word and image. It is possible that we might actually win the battle of words but lose the battle of images. And losing that battle could well cost us this generation.

Can a Renewal in Christian Worship Lead the Way to Renewal in the Arts?

One of the arguments I want to make is that, bewildering though this period of history is in so many ways, it offers some unique opportunities for Christian witness and spirituality—not only to renew themselves but in so doing to impact the larger culture. However tenuous may be the biblical and theological reflection behind some of the current renewal in worship, Christians (and churches) are taking much more seriously their call to this arena of cultural production, supporting artists working in the secular art world and the media, even encouraging the use of visual elements in worship. Meanwhile, the art world is experiencing its own turmoil and uncertainty. One of the important aspects of this upheaval is the breakdown of the walls between the various arts and between high and popular art. This has resulted in an environment that is much more open to creativity of all kinds, indeed to productions that call for interaction and community. Because of the popular influence on the production of art, spaces may be left open to expressions of creativity that allow for Christian perspectives and witness.

But there is an equally important reason why a renewal in Christian witness and worship could influence the larger culture. Beneath the glitter of popular visual culture, and clearly driving developments in the visual arts, is an unprecedented spiritual quest for reconciliation with each other and with the earth.[15] Moreover, in the arts, people seek a kind of summative experience in which they can discover meaning and purpose for their lives. The nature of deep aesthetic experiences is that they are ends in themselves; they have no practical goals outside themselves other than forcing people to take a break from their everyday lives and connect with whatever depths may exist. Indeed, for many modern people, aesthetic experience has replaced religious experience in providing an integrative vision of life.

Because of the developments just sketched, however, churches often appear imaginatively empty. Gerhard Richter, a contemporary German artist, expresses this poignantly: "Art is not a substitute for religion: it is a religion. The Church is no longer adequate as a means of affording experience of the transcendental, and of making religion real—and so art has been transformed from a means into the sole provider of religion."[16] Art is an experience of an artistic vision that is not a means to another end but is its own end. Simone Weil has argued that there are three ways people are drawn to God: through affliction, religious practices, and by the experience of beauty. The first two, she points out, have been virtually eliminated from modern life, leaving the third. Among white races, she argues, "The beauty of the world is almost the only way by which we can allow God to penetrate us."[17]

Art, then, may be a means, indeed one of the only means, that will catch the attention of this generation. The problem is that art by itself does not provide the reconciliation and spiritual connection that the human heart really longs for. It provides at best a kind of substitute religion. But when religion divests itself of all symbolism and imaginative depth, as it has in the minds of many of our contemporaries, art can appear to be the more attractive alternative. And artists and galleries often quite literally take on the role of spiritual sources. Listen to the way an art critic describes Michael Werner's remodeling of the famous Castelli gallery in New York, the scene of so many important shows in the history of modern art: "The heavy oak doors are still knobless and still open with a vigorous push; the hallway walls are still dark red, as are the thickly carpeted stairs, which still guarantee a suitably hushed, reverential ascent."[18] Such a setting surely suggests an experience that is in some important sense transcendent.

It is remarkable that the church and the experience of beauty and loveliness appear to be estranged and that the role of the church has been supplanted by art galleries (or theaters). The experience of worship—prayer, praise, and participation in the sacraments—provides for believers the opportunity of responding to the gracious presence of God with the whole of their beings. It is an embodied experience, involving standing, kneeling, or lifting of hands; it is a deeply emotional and intellectual response of the heart to God's offer of grace in Jesus Christ by the power of the Holy Spirit. But it is also an experience of the will as the believer gives up his or her life in service to God, by physically taking the bread and wine that is offered, or by going under the waters of baptism. Even such a brief description calls attention to the oral, visual, even kinesthetic dimensions of these experiences. These dimensions call for embodiment and performance that throughout Christian history have given birth to art—to singing, dancing, altarpieces, and, during the Middle Ages, to dramatic presentations.

It is impossible to write a history of art or architecture without pointing out the ways that Christian worship has influenced their development—though some modern writers have tried to do so. As noted above, this traditional connection has, since the Reformation, been damaged with respect to the visual arts, but as also noted, a revival of new forms of worship is currently underway. This revival has in part grown out of the revival of evangelical Christianity that has occurred since World War II. Beginning with the Youth for Christ rallies in the 1940s and continuing through the Jesus People in the 1970s, the practice of Christian worship has been undergoing a profound development that has led to the proliferation of the so-called seeker sensitive or "contemporary" worship services. It is not an exaggeration to note that this renewal has already begun to impact the larger culture.[19]

Clearly, this renewal in worship is itself being influenced by the surrounding popular culture, but this in itself is not a bad thing. Given a proper biblical and theological grounding, it is also possible that the renewal can in turn have an impact on that culture. Indeed, one of the characteristics of the evangelical forms of Christianity in America is its ability to shape, as well as be shaped by, the surrounding popular culture.[20] It is not difficult, of course, to point to examples of ways in which Christianity in America has simply been taken captive by the surrounding culture. As Steve Scott has argued, "Unless we are moving forward in seeking the genuine transformation of culture, then we are standing still and it is transforming us."[21] But one can also point to ways in which evangelical renewals have influenced culture. The current developments in worship, therefore, do not in themselves mean that a renewal in the arts is also underway; they only indicate that such a renewal is possible. But this can happen only if Christians learn to shape a worship experience that takes more seriously the depth of their Christian heritage and God's revelation in Scripture, as well as the call to a disciplined and mindful art. Is such a convergence too much to hope for? Before we can venture an answer, we have a great deal of ground to cover. In the next two chapters, I look in more detail at the ways that faith and art have interacted in Christian history. Following that, chapter 3 recalls biblical resources for practice and reflection on the arts. Chapter 4 explores possible theological frameworks for artistic practice. In chapter 5, I take stock in more detail of the current situation, and in chapter 6, I reflect on the opportunities and challenges it provides for Christians. In chapter 7, I reflect a bit on the practice and enjoyment of art itself to try to provide guidelines for its use (or potential abuse) by Christians. Finally, in the conclusion I again revisit the questions raised in this introduction.

development
of the visual arts
from the early church
to the middle ages

Christians of every age are tempted to feel that the challenges they face are unique, often associating this feeling with the fear that the world is somehow worse than it has ever been. In some ways the issues we face at the beginning of the new century *are* novel, especially in areas of technology and the prolif- eration of art forms and media. But other issues, such as tensions over the use of secular art forms and appropriate ways art can be used in the church, have reappeared throughout Christian history. It is important, therefore, before we consider the special challenges faced by twenty-first-century Christians, to briefly survey the ways Christians have used the visual arts in the past.

This chapter looks at the role the visual arts have played in the Christian tra- dition, paying special attention to the tensions and reforms such use has pre- cipitated. While there is a rich tradition of Christian use of art, various branches of Christianity have made different use of this heritage. In some cases, for long periods of time, segments of Christianity either ignored or despised the visual altogether. Therefore, part of the work of renewal in the arts, for contemporary Protestants at least, is an act of historical retrieval, as well as of biblical renewal.

I undertake such a survey not only for historical reasons, for the questions raised are more than simply historical in character. Since the church through- out its history was deeply concerned to defend and communicate the truth about God and the world, frequently, as we will see, discussions about the use of art were profoundly theological and only marginally about artistic elements. This is an important reminder, because it is all too easy to fall back on pragmatic or procedural reasons for either using or ignoring the visual. We need to bear in mind that these discussions imply critical concerns about our existence as God's image and the object of Christ's redemptive death. Indeed, it has been argued that the use of art might either support or undermine the very reality of, say, Christ's incarnation and the working of sacraments. How we answer questions about our visual culture, then, relates in critical ways both to our embodied life in the world and the obedience this entails, and to our call to worship God in spirit and in truth. I say a great deal more about these questions in chapter 3, but here we turn to some historical comments.

Early Christian Art and Worship

The visual culture of the early church had to be modest; indeed, the church itself was in many ways virtually invisible to outsiders. The reasons for this are not difficult to pinpoint. The small struggling congregations from the beginning faced misunderstanding, suspicion, even persecution. Until roughly A.D. 200 most visual imagery was found in catacombs, the burial places (and sometime hiding places) of Christians. Wall paintings contained shepherd images, fish symbols, and athletes' palms, and their presence was unobtrusive. Indeed, the meanings of such paintings were intentionally hidden from outsiders. As Paul Finney notes, "The signs and symbols that early Christians chose were illiative and mediated, not direct and unmediated."[1] One needed to know the meaning of the fish symbol, that its Greek letters spelled out Christ, God, Son, Savior. It was something only insiders would know and respond to. It was not intended—as it is today—to be a witness to outsiders. Indeed, specifically Christian symbols such as the cross seem to have been intentionally avoided by the early Christians. Instead, they borrowed generously from Greek imagery.[2] Christians from the beginning used this pagan vocabulary to express Christian sentiments, while carefully avoiding the humanistic connotations. The shepherd resembled Apollos but carried heavy biblical freight: The shepherd is Christ, these believers insisted, and he is my shepherd; therefore, I will not fear. An athlete's palm, the Greco-Roman reward for athletic victory, recalled Paul's reference to competing for the prize of the high calling of Christ.

In an important sense, these images assisted in the consolidation of the growing Christian communities. Crafted by anonymous artisans, they gave corporate expression to the faith of these communities—assisting in the development of what Dietrich Bonhoeffer called the discipline of the secret.[3] But at the same time it is clear that the images, culturally speaking, were never countercultural, even if their meanings decidedly were. This characteristic was to become decisive in the development of symbolism in the early church. The images' mediated quality meant that the objects—often borrowed from Greco-Roman art—

were not direct references to spiritual reality or spiritual truth but indirect ones. The viewer was supposed to look beyond the objects to the stories and reality that lay behind them.

In the third century, as Christianity became more established, marble imagery appeared, though it continued to portray the same images used by the early Christians. Interestingly, as Andre Grabar points out, marble imagery was clearly influenced by Greek funerary art, though any reference to death was missing.[4] Indeed, these images seem to be implicit prayers: Lord, save me as the shepherd saves the one lamb that was lost (see fig. 1); save me from my troubles as you saved Jonah (see fig. 2). These images embody the reality that early Christians felt of a divine power at work on their behalf. Though not necessarily made for a liturgical setting, their import is clearly devotional. These images are

Fig. 1. *The Good Shepherd,* Asia Minor, probably Phrygia (Central Turkey), c. 270–280. Marble, 50 x 25.7 x 15.9 cm. © The Cleveland Museum of Art, 2000, John L. Severance Fund, 1965.241. Used by permission.

particularly interesting because Christians in the early church were hesitant to use three-dimensional figures, perhaps for fear of making graven images. But in both these cases the emphasis is on the implied narrative, the scriptural story, to which these figures point. The use of figures to represent a narrative is called "abbreviated representation" and displays the indirect symbolism already described.

After the conversion of Constantine in 312, Christianity became the official religion of the Roman Empire, and Christian art and architecture were free to celebrate this triumph. Once Christianity was recognized (by the Edict of Milan in 313), buildings were built specifically as churches, and they were adorned with mosaics. Moreover, artists were employed to shape furnishings for religious

Fig. 2. *Jonah Cast Up*, Eastern Mediterranean, probably Asia Minor, Early Christian, c. 260–275. Marble, 40.6 x 21.6 x 37.6 cm. © The Cleveland Museum of Art, 2000, John L. Severance Fund, 1965.238. Used by permission.

uses, both private and public. Again, artists made use of Greek and Roman imagery that was common in secular art, but what they did with this vocabulary is striking.

A previous generation of scholars, represented in particular by Grabar and Ernst Kitzinger, argued that the iconography of this period was predominantly imperial. Taking over the imagery of Imperial Rome, these artists portrayed Christ as the new Emperor, communicating that he reigns over all, just as the earthly emperor reigns over the earthly political system. These scholars believed that the borrowing indicated a willingness to contextualize Christ's work within the impe-

Fig. 3. Detail of *Entry of Christ into Jerusalem*. Alinari/Art Resource, New York. Used by permission.

rial structure. But recently, Thomas Mathews has challenged this view, pointing out that while there are some superficial similarities between the Christian and secular art of this period, an important contest is really being carried on, what he calls a "clash of the gods." Christ challenges not only the power of the emperor but that of all other mediators of spiritual power. And he does this by subverting the expectations set up by contemporary imagery. In contrast to the coming of the emperor, Christ comes into Jerusalem riding on a humble donkey (as shown on the sarcophagus in fig. 3), sidesaddle (a decidedly nonmilitary posture!), almost feminine, making the lowly ass a collaborator of God's work.[5]

In fact, according to Mathews, this processional model is the closest thing to a program of imagery in the early church. In the very construction of church spaces and the images they contained—which would have been very public and visible to people—everyone was being invited to join the procession of saints and heavenly beings and to bring their gifts into the church and lay them at the feet of the Savior. As the tradition of the Eastern (or Byzantine) Church developed, this processional theology was central both to its liturgy and to its artistic program. Indeed, the images of this program anticipated the development of the icon. The processional theology can best be seen in the construction and mosaics of San Vitale in Ravenna (dedicated by Bishop Maximianus in A.D. 574), which was constructed on a central plan that focuses on a central apse, opening on to a domed space. The seven exedras—all decorated with mosaics of Old and New Testament figures—and the centrally placed altar all focus on the sacrifice of Christ. But on each side of the apse are large mosaics, on one side the Emperor Justinian and his courtiers, on the other Empress Theodora with her retinue (in Byzantine worship men and women always worshiped separately). The procession of the emperor is of particular interest, both for theological and political reasons (fig. 4). Notice that even as the figures process toward the altar (from

Fig. 4. *The Court of Justinian.* Foto Marburg/Art Resource, New York. Used by permission.

left to right), they face outward, confronting the viewer and underlining the presence of imperial authority. This frontal portraiture played an important role in the development of the icon, as we will see. Note too that the emperor, who dominates the scene, appearing taller than the rest (though in fact he was of average height), is preceded by three churchmen: two deacons, one with a censor, one holding a jeweled (Gospel) book, and a bishop identified in the inscription as Maximianus, who carries the processional cross. Following the emperor are two courtiers and a group of soldiers conspicuously displaying the Chi-Rho symbol (the first two Greek letters of the cross, which Constantine was supposed to have seen in the sky at his conversion). Justinian carries a golden bowl, which he brings as a gift to the altar.

Justinian's central, controlling location speaks of the two aspects of his power, both spiritual and political—symbolized by the churchmen in front and the soldiers and courtiers behind—for in the Eastern tradition the emperor rules in the place of God. So the panel is both a religious expression of faith in Christ and the honor that is due him—above this panel in the church, and the founder Saint Vitale is seen coming to a youthful Christ, who extends to him a crown of victory—and a political manifesto, which expresses the role of the emperor.

In all this Christ is not made to compete with the emperor, nor does he simply replace that rule, Mathews argues. His image is above that of the emperor.

Christ finds his place not among political rulers but among the gods of the ancient world. But unlike the gods, he plays many roles, and through the exercise of these roles, he gradually replaces these lesser gods. The struggle was not over iconography but ultimately about worship and service, with Christ gradually supplanting all claims to allegiance, whether divine or imperial.[6]

But as we have noted, the intent of these images was often hidden to the untrained eye. Their clarity, Grabar notes, "is a function of the training of the viewer."[7] Consider the ivory in the British Museum of the passion (fig. 5). This plaque, made perhaps for a wealthy home, is clearly meant to encourage instruction and remembrance. Here the full narrative of the betrayal and crucifixion is implied. Though the scene centers on Christ carrying his cross, on the left is Pilate, washing his hands, and to the right is Peter by the fire denying his Lord while the cock crows. Peter points to Christ, but the bystander points to Peter. Here the story is meant to inform, even inspire, and to recount and recall the biblical narrative, rather than evoke a spiritual reality. The spiritual intent is mediated to the viewer by the vocabulary of images that serve as abbreviated representations—a kind of shorthand for the full story of salvation.

At the same time, the aggressive building program of churches, begun in the fourth century by the wife of Constantine, opened up a larger liturgical setting for imagery. These worship spaces and their decoration, contrary to previous thinking, in no way competed with the teaching of the church fathers but rather

Fig. 5. Passion Scene. © The British Museum. Used by permission.

elaborated the teaching in ways that common people could understand and appreciate. Indeed, Margaret Miles argues that the universal appeal of these spaces and their imagery had an important theological impact. They showed at once the triumph of the church but also its universal embrace.[8] But because of their focus on the dramatic enactment of the liturgy, they also set the stage for subsequent controversies over the place and role of images.

Christians already recognized that while images could be useful in promoting appropriate worship, they were also dangerous. Not only were there the biblical warnings about idolatry, but there were also pagan and political connotations that needed to be avoided. As Mathews says of the struggles of the fourth and fifth centuries, "Images, no matter how discretely chosen, come freighted with conscious or subliminal memories; no matter how limited their projected use, they burn indelible outlines into the mind. . . . Images not only express convictions, they alter feelings and end up justifying convictions."[9] Though it may be difficult for our image-saturated generation to comprehend, this complex of issues would lead to some of the most bitter controversies in the church over the next thousand years.

During the next few centuries after Constantine, while it continued to develop its own symbolic imagery, the church also continued to borrow images and practices from the surrounding culture. Both practices became sources of controversy; in a sense, they became the points at which the Eastern and Western Church diverged in the eleventh century. As we will see, the Eastern Church did more to develop its own iconic vocabulary, while the Western Church did more to adapt images (and practices) from the surrounding culture. A most interesting promotion of the latter practice is found in a letter that Pope Gregory wrote to Augustine of Canterbury in the late sixth century. Augustine wondered about the culture of the Angles (in what is now England) and sought the advice of the pope. Gregory's letter reads in part:

> I have decided after long deliberation about the English people, . . . that the idol temples of that race should by no means be destroyed, but only the idols in them. Take holy water and sprinkle it in these shrines, build altars and place relics in them. For if the shrines are well built, it is essential that they should be changed from the worship of devils to the service of the true God. When this people see that their shrines are not destroyed they will be able to banish error from their hearts and be more ready to come to the places they are familiar with, but now recognizing and worshipping the true God. . . . It is doubt-less impossible to cut out everything at once from their stubborn minds: just as the man who is attempting to climb to the highest place, rises by steps and degrees and not by leaps.[10]

Notice the careful distinction between the idolatry practiced and the forms and buildings associated with it. Already one begins to see the emphasis, so important to later Christian practice, on the attitude of the heart and mind rather than on outward forms. Outward forms were meant to assist in forming godly habits of mind, and whatever was believed to contribute to this was welcomed. The Eastern Church, as we will see, took far more interest in the direct access to God that the forms provided, while the Western tradition placed greater emphasis on their pedagogical value.

The Iconoclastic Controversy and the Orthodox Image

This tradition of mediated images led both to the distinctive use of images in the West and to the controversy over the way images featured in worship in the East. To understand this development, we must return to the key voice in defining the Western medieval aesthetic, the earlier and more famous Augustine (d. 430), who came from Hippo in North Africa. It is important to note that Augustine reflected the Latin temperament of the West, which had always been more rational and analytic. Salvation was understood in terms of reconciliation with God through the cross, rather than as a spiritual communion with God (as in the East).

The single most important source for understanding the Western aesthetic is Augustine's *On Christian Doctrine* written in 396. God uses temporal things, he argued there, to show us the eternal reality for which our soul hungers— the earthly sign points to and represents a spiritual reality (though it does not directly mediate that reality). Echoing an openness to the surrounding culture, Augustine expressed the view that the world and Scripture are both full of signs that can lead us to God. A sign is a thing that causes us to think of something beyond the impression the thing itself makes on the senses, "so that by means of the corporal and temporal things, we may comprehend the eternal and spiritual."[11]

Central to this account is the death of Christ, which became especially significant in the Western artistic tradition. Augustine pointed out: "We ill used our immortality, so that we deserved to die; Christ used his mortality well to restore us. . . . He was willing to give his life for ours when he had power to take it up again."[12] Because Augustine was himself under the influence of Neoplatonic thinking, much here is similar to the Eastern view, as we shall see. The signs that God places in creation and Scripture are meant to lead us to a vision of God, where we will be like him, for we will see him as he is (1 John 3:2). But they do not do this directly; they are simply pointers. Moreover, there is a more calculated dependence on the work of Christ that is missing in Eastern thought—where it is the incarnation taken as a whole that saves rather than simply the death of Christ. Accordingly, there is a more pragmatic dependence on the objects of the sign in the West, what Augustine referred to as the "things." They are meant to point beyond themselves to the reality of God's work to which they refer.

As in the East, the saints—holy men and women, especially martyrs—in the West played a critical role. As Peter Brown points out, "The religious sensitivities of late antique men had long been molded by an intense dialogue with invisible companions."[13] But in the West this linkage was maintained more through an almost physical connection with the saint rather than through his or her image (what became the "icon" in the Eastern Church). Christians in the Western Church felt that the power of holy men and women was mediated through their remains or items from their lives, which had become signs. These remains or signs were called "relics," and they are crucial to understanding both the role of art in the West and the theological assumptions that drove its development. Relics became a symbol of the presence of God's power in and through the presence of the holy dead they represented. Shrines created to hold these relics, frequently containing altars, became centers of pilgrimages and made people more and more dependent on relics as the transmitters of God's power and forgiveness. As Brown describes this, the martyrs and their relics redrew the map that separated earth from heaven, for these objects not only reminded worshipers of supernatural reality but actually became a detached fragment of God's power. The arrival of a relic in a town, therefore, became an occasion of great celebration and worship. Brown describes, for example, the arrival in Rouen of the relics of St. Martin:

> By treating the arrival of [St. Martin's] relics as analogous to that of an emperor, [the Bishop] was not only emphasizing their invisible majesty; he was ensuring that their arrival would be an occasion for the Christians of Rouen to find room in their view of their own community, for a further category.[14]

That category is the universal power of God represented by the *praesentia* (presence) of the holy dead.

In the East by comparison, the images of Christ and the saints—what became known as "icons"—came to play a central role not only in liturgy but also in theology. To understand this development it is necessary to call attention to the writings of Dionysius, the Pseudo-Areopagite (so named because until the sixteenth century he was identified with Dionysius of Athens, whom Paul encountered in Acts 17), which combined a Neoplatonic view of the world with Christian doctrine. Dionysius wrote his *Celestial Hierarchy* in roughly A.D. 500, probably in Syria, in which he laid out a celestial and ecclesiastical hierarchy that defined the stages by which human nature is "deified" (*theosis*, divinization, or becoming Godlike, in Eastern theology). The idea of this divinization came from Athanasius, who in the fourth century had described the work of Christ in his treatise *On the Incarnation*. There Athanasius argued that it was by the incarnation, that is, the taking on of human flesh, that God accomplished the renewal of creation. Christ became human, Athanasius argued, so that we might become (like) God.

Dionysius further described this spiritual process, mediated through the nine orders of angels, by which humanity can progressively become like God. The goal of this journey to God is the union of the soul with God, and it is achieved by a process of "unknowing, in which the soul leaves behind the perceptions of the senses as well as the reasoning of the intellect."[15] This mystical theology had much influence on both Eastern and Western Christianity, but it became dominant in the worldview of Eastern orthodoxy.

Art, then, in churches influenced by this vision was meant to lift the soul toward the contemplation of God, to stimulate, as Bernard McGinn put it, a "contemplative movement from the perceptible 'up' to the conceptual."[16] Images, or icons, were placed before the worshiper to excite the one praying to love and imitate the one portrayed, that is, to turn away from a worldly love toward a purer love of God. But these images did more than simply recall or represent the reality behind them, as images did in the West; in an important sense they became bearers of this reality. They became the equivalent of relics in the West.

Gervase Mathew describes three steps in the development of icons.[17] The first stage is found in the veneration of the imperial image, which was placed in significant places throughout the empire (as seen in the mosaic of Justinian). As the emperor's image represented the presence of the emperor, Christ's image, or the image of a saint, came to serve as a kind of "proxy" for their presence. Such images assisted, then, in the veneration of these holy persons. Neoplatonism certainly played a role here with its view of the transparency of the image. Venerating the image was not a veneration of the object but the person who was visible in and through the image. The image did not simply represent the one portrayed but actually became transparent; that is, one could see through the image to the sacred presence it represented. The figure of Christ seen in the ivory wing of a diptych from the mid-sixth century (fig. 6) is an example of this stage. Here Christ frontally confronts the viewer as he holds up his hand to bless. Notice the figure's iconic quality, that is, its tendency to fill the frame and even push itself out of that frame. The figure gradually takes on a greater importance than the narrative in which it is embedded.

The second stage involved the rise of the use of funerary imagery in private devotions. Some of these images of holy people worked miracles on behalf of the worshiper, and thus a cult of images (analogous to the cult of relics in the West) began to grow. Shrines or churches built to house the images often became a center for worship and, eventually, a destination of pilgrimages.

The third stage occurred at the end of the seventh century, when portraits or images of Christ and the saints began to appear as isolated frontal figures. Perhaps, Mathew surmises, this allowed the image to confront the viewer and thus be more easily invoked. By the beginning of the eighth century it had become common practice to venerate these images, which meant that honor paid to the image honored the person represented there.

An important event connected to these developments was a council held in Trullo in A.D. 692, which actually repudiated the earlier symbolic art of the church

Fig. 6. Figure of Christ Enthroned. Foto Marburg/Art Resource, New York. Used by permission.

in favor of the icon. The eighty-second canon of this council reveals the clearest indication of the growing division between the Eastern and Western traditions. Symbolic representations of Christ as the Lamb, for example, were forbidden. The reason for this was that the Lamb was a "typos" or figure of the coming of grace, which was truly and fully realized in Christ. Signs were to be respected, the canon reasoned, but priority belonged to the truth of which the sign was a type. Therefore, the council prescribed that Christ should be depicted as a man in remembrance of his actual incarnation, passion, and the universal redemption available in him.[18] Not only did this decision repudiate the symbolic quality of earlier Christian art but also its fundamental narrative intent, and even more its historical orientation. Here the divergence between East and West can be clearly seen. The central image of Eastern Christianity became the human figure, represented in its timeless quality in the icon.[19] Meanwhile, the central image of Western Christianity became Jesus suffering on the cross, paying the price for human sin. As a result, images that articulated this reality, such as the image of the Lamb or the chalice, proliferated in the West during the Middle Ages.

The practice in the East of venerating the image of Christ inevitably caused those accustomed to a more symbolic orientation to react. Christians who opposed the use of images in worship generally felt that these objects marginalized the work of Christ and especially the worshipers' participation in Christ through the Eucharist, which was, to the iconoclasts, a better "relic" of Christ than his image.

In 730, Emperor Leo III represented these interests by destroying images of Christ, his mother, and the saints. And for a generation the iconoclast party held control. In October 787, supporters of icons, called the iconodules, came to power and defined the orthodox position on images. As the Second Council of Nicaea, convened by the Empress Irene, stated in 787, icons, wherever they were to be found, were to be venerated, "for the more often they are seen in their pictorial representations, the more the beholder is excited to the recollection and desire of the ones represented, and to offer them greeting and reverent worship."[20] John of Damascus, the most famous theologian of orthodoxy, believed that critical theological issues were at stake, specifically the true humanity of Christ. He wrote, "When he who is bodiless and without form, immeasurable in the boundlessness of his own nature, existing in the form of God, empties himself and is found in a body of flesh, then you may draw his image and show it to anyone willing to gaze upon it."[21] Icons displayed and insisted on the full humanity of Christ. They should not only be allowed but stipulated. What is called in the East the triumph of orthodoxy (still celebrated as a special feast day) was the reinstatement of images in the churches. Their use was not optional precisely for theological reasons: They followed from the full and complete humanity of the God-man. As John said, "When he who was bodiless [becomes bodily] . . . then you may draw his image and gaze upon it."[22]

The icon, therefore, was much more than an aesthetic image to grace the church and stimulate holy thoughts. It was something that expressed deeply held theological convictions, and it was meant to move the viewer to love and serve God. In many respects, an icon was theology in a visual form, and the practice of making an icon in itself represented a spiritual discipline—to be accomplished with much prayer and spiritual preparation. As John of Damascus insisted in his defense of icons, this use of images was stipulated from the beginning as a part of holy devotion, and they belong not to artists but to the holy fathers of the church. The orthodox use of images was more than the triumph of popular religion over imperial edict; it was a reaffirmation of what, to these theologians, was an ancient tradition dating back to Christ and his apostles.

The program that developed around the use of icons is perhaps best seen during the so-called second golden age of Byzantine art, the eleventh century. One of the best surviving examples of this period is the church at Daphni just outside Athens, dating from the late eleventh century. At Daphni the centrally organized design focuses on the large central apse, where the image of Christus Pantocrator appears (fig. 7). Here at the top of the dome is the risen and reigning Christ, which constitutes the central image of the iconographical program of the church. Christ's image is the image of the eschatological rule and glory of God, who is made accessible to the believer by participation in the worship of his people in this sacred space.

Fig. 7. *Christ the Almighty (Pantocrator)*. Foto Marburg/Art Resource, New York. Used by permission.

The squinches below the dome contain mosaics of the annunciation, nativity, baptism, and transfiguration, each connected with rays reaching toward the central image of Christ—the source of the power (or energy as it is called in the East) demonstrated and revealed in these events. The focus again is on incarnation and glorification as the images central to salvation. The incarnation is the event that takes up the fallen creation into the divine being. The narrative elements are suppressed; the entry into Jerusalem and even the crucifixion and resurrection are allocated to the transept arms adjoining the apse.

While the division was long and gradual, and the reasons complicated, in 1054 the Western and Eastern Churches officially split, separating Rome and Constantinople. As noted above, however, the imaginative worlds, and the theology behind them, had been diverging for many centuries. The division marked a low point in the life of the Western Church and its impact on the surrounding culture. The Byzantine tradition, of which the Eastern Church was a part, was to have periodic influence on the developing Western tradition (especially via Venice, which maintained continuing relations with the East).

Western Art and Faith from the Eleventh to the Sixteenth Century

Around 1200 a stirring began in France that initiated a period known as the Early Renaissance. During this period a renewal in the arts was closely connected with reform movements that began springing up throughout western Europe. Already in the eleventh century, Gregory VII (d. 1085) and Anselm (d. 1109), Archbishop of Canterbury, had worked to reform the clergy and reinforce clerical celibacy.

In the middle of the twelfth century, a group of monks intent on reforming the church settled in France, in the Île-de-la-cité (a section of Paris). There they built a church that would become the predecessor of Notre Dame Cathedral. Making use of methods developed by Abott Suger in his church of St. Denis (dedicated in Paris in 1144), they built a structure that featured for the first time the soaring arches, tracery, and "curtain walls" of the Gothic style. Partly a result of advances in engineering (which accompanied advances in many fields in the twelfth century), so-called flying buttresses were able to support very thin walls and stained-glass windows, which were able to reach a great height, as seen in the nave of the cathedral at Reims (fig. 8), leading worshipers to lift their eyes to the mystical spaces above.

But the theological significance of Gothic cathedrals was, if anything, equally striking, for the structure of the buildings, especially as it was embodied in the great cathedrals of Strasbourg (1220) and Reims (1230), became a concrete expression of the holistic worldview of the church that was being recovered by the early reform movements. These great structures, which must have been extremely impressive amid the modest buildings around them, not only became the center of the social and religious life of the community but were actually intended to be a microcosm of the world at large. An image of the last judgment was frequently located over the central portal of the cathedral (see, for example, the portal at Ameins in fig. 9), reminding those entering of God's certain judgment, which was avoided only by entering and eating the holy food of the Eucharist. The space of the church represented the "ark of salvation."[23] On either side of the central portal were

Fig. 8. Nave of Reims Cathedral. Giraudon/Art Resource, New York. Used by permission.

Fig. 9. *The Last Judgment,* Amiens Cathedral. Foto Marburg/ Art Resource, New York. Used by permission.

images of the prophets and apostles, on whose word rested the hope of God's people. Inside the worshiper was drawn both forward and upward toward the altar, placed at the central and raised position, where the body and blood of Christ, the bread of heaven and the cup of salvation, were distributed.[24] The sculptured figures and scenes, the light cast on the altar, even the space itself were all shaped to give expression to the teachings of the church. Together they represented a unified worldview that encompassed every creature and all ages of Christian history. In medieval symbolism, this fullness or plenitude of meaning was the medieval equivalent of the later Renaissance understanding of perspective—it controlled the entire structure much like perspective would later control a visual space. All of reality, as Augustine had said, was made into a symbol of the (real) spiritual world, an *analogia entis* (analogy of being).[25]

The reawakening of faith during this period of time was embodied, and also stimulated, by the major mendicant movements (so-called because, initially at least, they depended on alms for their living) that were founded early in the thirteenth century. Two in particular would have a great influence on the development of the arts and, indeed, on much of the cultural life of the Middle Ages. At the turn of the century, Francis of Assisi (1181/82–1226), while worshiping, heard the Lord speak the words of Matthew 10 to his disciples: "Cure the sick, raise the dead, cleanse lepers, cast out demons. You received without payment; give without payment. Take no gold, or silver, or copper in your belts" (vv. 8–9). Feeling this was a personal call from God, Francis discarded his staff and even his shoes, put on a dark robe tied with a rope, and set out to preach and save souls. He soon gathered followers, and in 1209, the Franciscan order was approved by Pope Innocent III. In 1220, St. Dominic of Spain (1170–1221), dissatisfied with the lax Christian faith he saw around him, founded the Dominican order with the mission to preach the true faith and defend the church against heretics and infidels. (A third movement, the Cistercians, would also prove influential in later fifteenth-century art. This order of "White Monks" was founded in 1098 as a stricter and purified form of the Benedictines, whom these reformers felt had lost their original vision.)

Francis's break with the social and ecclesiastical structures symbolized an even more significant revolution in imagination and feeling. Francis was known for his mystical identification with every creature of God, and the order he founded sought simplicity of feeling for God and the world. More than any other factor, this awakening of feeling and genuine faith revived medieval culture. Erich Auerbach has insisted that Francis "was the first to awaken the dramatic powers of Italian feeling and language."[26] His influence was most profound in the developing tradition of mystical theology, represented by St. Bonaventure, who became the Minister General of the Franciscan order in 1257. Following the ideas of Dionysius examined earlier, he taught that all human wisdom is folly when compared with the mystical illumination that God accords his faithful followers.

The transformation of the imagination that resulted was so far-reaching that John Dixon has claimed it was "the indispensable first step in the western intellectual enterprise."[27] Its influence is seen, for example, in the most famous of Francis's artist followers, Giotto di Bondone (d. 1337). In the passion series for the Arena Chapel in Padua, Giotto captured this awakening both of human feeling and the related awareness of real pictorial space. In the *Deposition* (fig. 10), the tender cradling of the dead Christ is placed low in the space, adding to the emotional impact, but it all takes place within a real space and on solid ground. We feel that we are actual participants in the drama portrayed. The people (and even the angels above) are all participating in a dramatic activity of great significance, but one that the viewer is invited to share. The low center of gravity also gives the impression that the space of the picture and our space is continuous. Giotto has created a new space, Dixon notes, which the worshiper contemplates from his or her own space.[28] He concludes, "For the first time . . . we find depicted the fully developed person acting to some moral purpose toward coherent and understandable ends."[29] But here too is a further development of the narrative interest noted in the earlier Christian art of the West.

The significance of both a narrative approach and real-life settings can be underlined by recalling the role the icon played in Eastern Christianity. An icon was not simply a reminder of the person invoked but a means by which the worshiper could access the divine reality. In the West, by contrast, images occupied real space, creating a stimulus for devotion. This is exemplified by the fact that the narratives of the biblical tradition, especially the life of Christ, formed

Fig. 10. *The Deposition,* Giotto di Bondone. Alinari/Art Resource, New York. Used by permission.

the center of medieval art in the West. Images of Christ's life and death, which accomplished the divine transaction, re-enacted through the Eucharist, brought the worshiper into communion with God.

This is further illustrated in a wonderful altarpiece by Guariento di Arpo (1310–1370), the closest of Giotto's immediate followers, from roughly 1344 (fig. 11). This early panel painting was made to stand behind the altar in a chapel dedicated to the assumption of Mary. Interestingly, the development of panel painting designed for placement behind the altar reflects liturgical developments in the church. "In the 13th c. the priest began to celebrate Mass from the front of the altar, his back facing the congregation. This change, intended to enhance the mystery of the Eucharist by shielding it from view, opened up the space at the back of the altar for art."[30] The first panel paintings were made to fill this space. But notice the narrative emphasis of this splendid work. Though the background is gold, indicating that these events have an eternal significance, the people move freely in real space, a space that again opens out into that of the viewer. Though many of the events of Christ's life are recounted, the images of his death and resurrection hold primary importance, a fact emphasized by the central position of the crucifix at the top of the altar.

Meanwhile, the Dominican friars sought to instruct the church through the preaching of the true faith. The most famous Dominican was a contemporary of Bonaventure, St. Thomas Aquinas (1225–1274), whose massive *Summa* has been compared to a written cathedral, encompassing the totality of medieval dogma. In many ways, Thomas shared the dominant medieval worldview, which was still based on a Neoplatonic framework. It could perhaps best be described as a spirituality of ascent, whereby a worshiper progressively ascends, first through the exercise of reason, and finally through prayer and meditation. The goal of the spiritual life was the "beatific vision," which could not be experienced fully until heaven but which could be anticipated through various mystical experiences. Indeed, Thomas himself the week before his death had a vision of God while worshiping, causing him to assert that, by comparison with this vision, all he had written was worthless.

Fig. 11. *Coronation of the Virgin Altarpiece,* Guariento di Arpo, 1344. Tempera and gold leaf on panels (32), 86 x 104³/₈" overall. © Norton Simon Art Foundation, Pasadena, California. Used by permission.

This view of the Christian life as a spiritual ascent through the trials of life to the beatitude of heaven found its highest expression in Dante Alighieri's (1265–1321) *Divine Comedy* (1314), which had a great influence on subsequent visual art. Dante had studied with the Dominicans in Florence and sought to represent faithfully Aquinas's views. One of the first pieces of literature written in vernacular Italian, *The Divine Comedy,* describes Dante's journey up from the Inferno, through Purgatorio, to Paradiso, led in turn by Virgil, who represents human reason, Beatrice, symbolizing divine love, and finally by Bernard of Clairvaux, one of the most famous Cistercian mystical theologians. The trilogy ends with a vision of God in heaven, where Dante "stared fixed and motionless upon that vision ever more fervent to see in the act of seeing," and he learns "how our image merges into that circle and how it there finds place."[31]

In the fourteenth century, the influences of the Franciscans and Dominicans converged with artistic influences from Northern Europe, helping to create the style known as International Gothic. The Cistercian influence (and St. Bernard in particular) was especially important. Timothy Verdon says of this impulse, "The charmingly human Madonnas with their jocund or solemn infants, the bleeding Christs and plangent Pietas that make up so great a part of fourteenth century sculpture and painting all owe a debt to Bernard and to the wider Cistercian influence."[32] The International style also combined emotional impact (awakened by Francis and stimulated by the first and most severe outbreak of the plague in 1348) with the increasing preoccupation with narrative. The lovely *Adoration of the Magi* by Gentile da Fabriano (c. 1370–1427) (pl.1) especially illustrates the decorative detail, the rich color, and the lyrically linear manner of the International Gothic, which might properly be called the last of the medieval movements. The scene focuses not on the holy family but on the kings who have come to pay tribute to the child-king. The one in the center holds up his gift, while his friend bows before the Christ child, who reaches out a hand in blessing. People crowd around to join with the Magi in honoring this birth. Note especially the procession in the distance that moves toward what is surely the heavenly city, taking into it, as St. John says, the "glory and the honor of the nations" (Rev. 21:26). God the Father is placed above, between images of the annunciation and the prophets who foretold the birth of Christ, while the dove, representing the Spirit, hovers between the Father and the Son. In a way that parallels the great cathedrals, altarpieces of this time reflect the full narrative of Scripture, in which this event finds its meaning.

If the Franciscan influence was dominant in the early years of the Renaissance, the later Renaissance owed much of its existence to key painters who expressed the theology and spirituality of the Dominican tradition—especially those who represented the renewal movement of that order, the so-called "observants" (*osservanzas*).[33] In Florence in the Dominican Sta. Maria Novella, the artist Masaccio (1401–1428), in 1425, painted his fresco *Trinity with the Virgin and St.*

Fig. 12. *Trinity with the Virgin and St. John,* Massacio. Alinari/Art Resource, New York. Used by permission.

John (fig. 12). Masaccio continued what Giotto had begun a hundred years before, except that his figures have more human shape, and the space (and perspective) is even more scientifically accurate. But notice that these innovations, important as they are in their own right, are clearly subordinated in Masaccio's mind to the theological reality he is portraying. The space, for example, is articulated, and the space of God the Father, the dove, and Christ, a space that Mary and John share, is clearly distinguished from that of the donor family, the Lenzi (whose tomb is below the picture). The family's sphere, in

Fig. 13. *The Annunciation,* Fra Angelico. Foto Marburg/Art Resource, New York. Used by permission.

turn, is separated from our own as observers of this scene. But the inscription over the tomb draws the connection between them and us: "What you are I was; what I am you will be." But the connection both within the Trinity and between the Trinity and us is also evident. The intimacy within the Trinity is wonderfully expressed as God holds up the arms of the cross, bearing up, as it were, the suffering body of the Son. That this space is not ultimately separated from us is indicated by the way the vanishing point of the vault in which the Trinity resides joins at the point of the floor on which the Lenzi family stands. The construction and interaction of the spaces suggest that this wondrous event—in which all members of the Trinity participate—is inextricably connected with our world, and this death connects with our own space and becomes the ground for our hope.

Across Florence in San Marco, an Observant Dominican monastery (a renewed form of the order that sought to more closely follow Dominic's rules), Fra Angelico (1400–1455) worked faithfully for many years on frescoes that decorated the public rooms and the cells of the monastery. Fra Angelico added an emotional depth and pathos to the theology his order espoused. In his *Annunciation* (fig. 13), Fra Angelico integrated the spatial innovations of Masaccio along with that painter's dignity and order. But to these he added a humility and simplicity that was unique to the "Blessed Angelico." He is known to have taken his vows very seriously and painted in a way that would encourage others in the life of prayer. His work may lack some of the later sophistication of the Renaissance, but it more than makes up for this in its combination of simple directness and deeply felt faith.

During the time Angelico was working on these frescoes, he was invited to Orvieto to do drawings for an ambitious cycle of frescoes for the cathedral of that city. Before he had time to complete this massive work, he died, and the cathedral chapter asked Luca Signorelli (1470?–1523) to complete the work. Just as the sixteenth century dawned, Signorelli completed the cycle of frescoes that is one of the most ambitious of the Renaissance period. Indeed, Signorelli's frescoes bear a definite resemblance to Michelangelo's work in the Sistine Chapel, which they clearly influenced.[34] The frescoes portray the overthrow of the Antichrist, whose false preaching is opposed by the faithful preaching of Dominican friars; the end of the world; and the resurrection of the flesh.

The fresco of *The Resurrection of the Flesh* (fig. 14) is important on a number of levels. First, it was painted just two years after the radical Dominican Savanarola (Abott of San Marco in Florence) was put to death. One of the objects of that radical reformer's wrath was the increasingly common practice of painting nudes and pagan subjects. Here Signorelli quite intentionally incorporates

Fig. 14. *The Resurrection of the Flesh,* Luca Signorelli. Alinari/Art Resource, New York. Used by permission.

Fig. 15. *Madonna and Child with a Book,* Raffaello Sanzio called Raphael, c. 1502–1503. Oil on panel, 21³/₄ x 15³/₄". © Norton Simon Art Foundation, Pasadena, California. Used by permission.

nude bodies in his portrayal of the resurrection. His starting point is surely St. Paul's reference in 1 Corinthians 15 that at the last trumpet the dead in Christ will be raised in incorruptible bodies. But as Margaret Miles points out, there is clearly another source for Signorelli's work, St. Augustine's *City of God*. In book XXII, Augustine contrasts the damnation of those who cling to the transitory world with those who fix their love on God. At the resurrection "all defects will be removed from those bodies, yet their essential nature will be preserved," and "we shall enjoy one another's beauty for itself alone."[35] Signorelli then follows Augustine in asserting that the perfection of life in heaven is embodied, graphically indicated by his portrayal of those being raised, struggling up out of the graves and gradually taking on bodily form. Figures touch and converse lovingly, enjoying their bodily existence, which as Augustine put it, is "without use." Despite the attempts of Savanarola, it is clear from Michelangelo's work a generation later that this view survived. But this visual hermeneutics of Scripture (and a church father) would be overruled in the Counter Reformation. In 1563, the Council of Trent forbade the portrayal of unsuitable objects. This was immediately interpreted as a ban on nudity in paintings, and as a result, many of Michelangelo's nudes were subsequently clothed.

But in the interim Signorelli's interpretation won out; indeed, it is possible to say that the nude body became a central symbol of the High Renaissance. One reason for this was the recovery of the breadth of Christian tradition—in this case, the writings of Augustine. But another source was the humanists who were influenced in the fifteenth century by a fresh reading of the newly translated writings of Plato. In mid century, Cosimo de Medici invited Marsilio Ficino to found an academy in Florence that would make the city into a new Athens. Ficino taught that the human figure occupied a central position between heaven and earth. By turning toward earthly love, one could descend to a lower state, or by turning in love toward God, one could ascend to his likeness. The body, therefore, was central—it could lead one toward or away from God.

Renaissance imagery of the incarnation obviously made use of this teaching, as is illustrated by an exquisite Madonna of Raphael (1483–1520) painted in 1503–1504 (fig. 15). The realistic portrayal of human forms, clothing, and figures in a real space has been developed to the highest level. Note that the Madonna is set within a contemporary setting in Raphael's native Italy, rather than in the timelessness of eternity. The structure of the composition is typical of the High Renaissance, built on a series of triangles, expressive of the mathematical order called the "golden section" (based on the isosceles triangle). Renaissance theorists and artists felt this proportionality gave a sense of peace and stability to their work.

But once again these formal qualities have been put into the service of the theological assertion the artist wishes to make. First, the baby sits unclothed at his mother's breast. This fact had been much observed but little analyzed until Leo Steinberg wrote a book called *The Sexuality of Christ*.[36] Steinberg argued that the frequent nude portrayal of Christ was not simply a Renaissance preoccupation with the body but a theological assertion of the highest importance. It was an insistence that the appearance of God in human form, rather than merely a mythological story, was an actual and visible fact. Christ became a real human being, as one can observe by looking at this nude body. This theological (and devotional) intent was further emphasized by the interaction between the child and the mother. The mother looks lovingly down at the child, while the latter, who must be about his Father's business, looks up past his mother as though into heaven. Meanwhile, he holds up to her a prayer book that is opened to the service called nones. This service, celebrated at three o'clock in the afternoon, recalls the death of Christ, who is said to have died at three in the afternoon on Good Friday. Christ's humanity is real, and though he is the object of the deep love of his mother, his coming death will be real too and will pierce her heart. He came into the world as a real human figure and died the death that all humans die, but with a different end—that of resurrection.

development
of the visual arts
from the reformation
to the twenty-first
century

While the history and traditions of the medieval period are an important part of the Christian heritage, it was the Reformation that gave birth to the particular challenges and tensions that characterize the modern world—especially in regard to Christians and their relationship to the arts. We begin our discussion of the modern world, then, with a consideration of the Reformation.

Reformations and the Reformation

The previous chapter revealed the influences of reform movements in the church on art and culture. This might appear to be a one-sided view of things, for much of the church, and the art that was produced both inside and outside the church, remained, to the thinking of many, unreformed. Take, for instance, the story of Martin Luther's visit to Rome in the early 1500s and his observation of the superstition (and extravagance) associated with images and relics, and the practices of people who made use of these things. Indeed, Luther is supposed to have said that St. Peter's itself was "built with the flesh, skin, and bones of the flock." Still, this view is what I call the default description of the Renaissance. There were, in fact, many who for centuries sought diligently to reform the church. And arguably, these reform movements had as much if not more influence on the development of art at this time as did the dominant (and one is tempted to say dormant) traditions of the church.

While the Renaissance was flourishing in Italy, in the North, groups such as the Brethren of the Common Life, with their emphasis on prayer, biblical study, and education, sought to return the church to its original commitments. Thomas à Kempis (1380–1471) and Rudolph Agricola (1443–1485) are perhaps the best known of the Brethren, the former for his famous *Imitation of Christ*, which has become a classic description of the spiritual life.

When one reads Thomas's description of the Christian life, one is struck immediately with its modest self-sacrificing focus on prayer and the service of God and neighbor. From what one reads there, one would not find much to support an elaborate artistic (or architectural) program. In book III, chapter 54, he contrasts natural inclinations with those arising from grace:

> Nature dreads shame and contempt; but grace rejoices to suffer reproach for the name of Jesus. Nature loves ease and bodily repose; but grace cannot be idle, and embraces labor gladly. Nature seeks to have things that are curious and beautiful, and abhors such as are cheap and coarse. But grace delights in what is plain and humble, does not reject coarse things, or refuse to be clad in old garments.[1]

Indeed, in reading Thomas's view of the Christian life, I have thought repeatedly of the art of Rembrandt or Jacob van Ruisdael. In one sense, this spiritual tradition promoted, long before the Reformation, a tradition that was hardworking, humble, and in an important sense not conducive to the production of what we would call the fine arts. It is possible to argue that, in a sense, when the Reformation reached the North, it occupied a cultural space that already existed. The Reformation may have encouraged a certain habit of thought in the North, but it did not necessarily create it.[2]

According to this view, culturally speaking, the Reformers resonated with certain elements of existing medieval traditions and opposed others. Both John Calvin (1509–1564) and Martin Luther (1483–1546), for example, preferred a nominalist and mystical way of thinking about God that owed a great deal to the medieval mystical tradition. This tradition sought simplicity and focused on inward and individual piety. Luther was more open to the use of images in worship and in private devotion, based on his emphasis on justification by faith. Once one is justified one is free to use images if they are helpful; on the other hand, if one does not believe, no image will help.

Calvin in this area as in so many others was more direct. He attacked in particular the views of Gregory the Great (the sixth-century pope mentioned earlier), especially his insistence that images were the books of the uneducated. To the contrary, Calvin noted, "Whatever men learn of God in images is futile, indeed false, the prophets totally condemn the notion that images stand in the place of books."[3] By contrast, it is through the pure preaching of the Word that one comes to proper faith. "In the preaching of his Word and sacred mysteries [God] has bidden that a common doctrine be there set forth for all. But those whose eyes rove about in contemplating idols betray that their minds are not diligently intent upon this doctrine."[4] What is this doctrine? It is the pure preaching of the Word of Scripture. Calvin stated, "Christ is depicted before our eyes as crucified. . . . From this one fact they could have learned more than from a thousand crosses of wood and stone."[5] Calvin is not saying that one sort of image ought to replace another. Rather, he is saying that there is a higher and more direct way of grasping what is true than by the use of images—an inward faith in the preached Word. Only in this way can God's true majesty be grasped, by a faculty that is "far above the perception of our eyes. . . . Even if the use of images contained nothing evil, it still has no value for teaching."[6]

But do images have no value? Even if one were to insist that the higher way of knowing is through the grasp of verbal preaching internally, could one not also grant that images support or, indeed, enrich this knowing? Calvin himself seems to indicate that this might be possible, for he waxes eloquent on the beauty of the world and the way God shows himself to us there, as though it were a kind of theater for God's glory. "Let us not be ashamed to take pious delight in the works of God open and manifest in this most beautiful theatre,"[7] and "There is no spot in the universe wherein you cannot discern at least some sparks of his glory. You cannot in one glance survey this most beautiful system of the universe in its wide expanse without being completely overwhelmed by the boundless force of its brightness."[8]

But when it comes to worship, it seems, there is no place for the visual. In worship it is the preached Word of God that gives entrance to God's grace. But does Calvin's theology actually forbid all use of images or only the abuse of such use? One might argue, though I will not do so here, that while Calvin seems to have forbidden all use of images in worship, his theology does not support such an extreme position (though his followers usually read him that way!). Whatever his intention, his views, especially as interpreted by his followers, have become decisive in subsequent Protestant—especially Reformed—practice.

Whatever Calvin's true view of images, his views of faith and the way faith lays hold on truth is indisputable. I would argue that the change he introduces here is fundamentally one of imagination, that is, the way the mind grasps and articulates reality. This change did not take place all at once, of course, for we have observed ways in which this move was anticipated. Indeed, some have argued that this path can be traced back as far as Augustine, and, to be fair, to the apostle Paul himself.[9]

It is in this context that one should understand the various "iconoclastic" movements of the Reformation. At various times people were moved to break into churches and destroy the images and statues that had proliferated at the end of the medieval period. These stirrings were not simply a desire to destroy art expressed by people who could not appreciate its beauty. Deeper motives were at work. On the one hand, there was the awareness that financial resources that could have been used to help the poor were being used instead to create decorations. On the other hand, people felt that the images represented a corrupt and superstitious order that needed to be deconstructed. But these acts of destruction were also carried out in the light of a new inner orientation of faith and worship that formed the center of the Reformers' preaching.

In its simplest form, the Reformation—and Calvin in particular—introduced (or at least encouraged) a change from an objective to a personal piety. Think of medieval worshipers going on a pilgrimage or to a shrine of a saint. They said their rosary there and paid homage, but it wasn't important that they felt anything special while they were there (though many no doubt did). These experiences were always communal and dramatic; they testified, in John Drury's words, to the "socially cohesive power of physical totems in religious life"[10] Images, practices, and communal liturgy obviously were critical to the religion of this period. By the time of the Reformation, fed by streams from medieval mysticism and the writings of people such as Thomas à Kempis, faith had become more specifically "personal," consisting of an inward cleaving to Christ and his promises. This, of course, involved the application of the mind and did not require visual meditation. Here we touch on a development that in some ways marked the turning from the medieval to the modern world, where, as Margaret Miles argues, people come to privilege "subjective consciousness as the normative human activity."[11]

Accompanying this turn were certain cultural developments, chief among which were the printing press and the appearance of Scripture in the vernacular. It would be impossible to imagine the Reformation apart from the cultural opportunities that the Reformers exploited. At the same time, these innovations worked together to develop a particular form of piety and an accompanying worship experience, which included sitting in pews, closing one's eyes during prayers, and so on. In such a setting, images necessarily played no role; in fact, they were usually perceived as a distraction from the inward focus on the preached (and sung) Word.

This is not to say that these developments did not have important positive significance in many areas of culture. This atmosphere, however, whatever its virtues, clearly placed a handicap on those who sought to give religious meaning to physical objects or to visual art. We can, following Calvin, find delight in creation and see there the hand of God, who alone deserves our worship, but we must not make it or any image of it a part of our liturgy. The "acts" or "works" of liturgy (which means literally the work of the people) in the Reformed tradition have centered and revolved around the proclamation of the Word. Any visual artifact, even any architectural worship space, was subservient to this central preoccupation. Charles Garside's summary of the position of Ulrich Zwingli, a contemporary of Calvin, sums up the reformers' views nicely: "The prime symbol of true belief is the word, invisible and heard; the prime symbol of false belief is the image, visible and seen."[12]

Consider, for example, the proliferation of woodcuts and broadsheets during the Reformation. During the time of tension between the Reformers and Rome, these art forms became popular media used to support and illustrate the preaching of the Reformers (though as in the case of Albert Dürer they could achieve a very high quality). Rather than serving some higher theological purpose, however, as art typically did before the Reformation, these woodcuts and

Fig. 16. *The Raising of Lazarus,* Rembrandt van Rijn. Gift of H. F. Ahmanson and Company, in memory of Howard F. Ahmanson. Photograph © Museum Associates/LACMA.

Fig. 17. *Three Trees in a Mountainous Landscape with a River,* Jacob van Ruisdael, c. 1665–1670. Oil on canvas, 54³/₈ x 68¹/₈". © Norton Simon Foundation, Pasadena, California. Used by permission.

broadsheets served the more practical purpose of supporting the message of the Reformers. They were auxiliary to the work of preaching.

Alternatively, woodcuts, and much art that was made in England and Holland, was a kind of visual interpretation of Scripture. Indeed, Protestant art that interpreted Scripture dominated the visual arts in that tradition. In Rembrandt's (1606–1669) *Raising of Lazarus* (fig. 16), the artist has captured the moment when Christ said, "Lazarus, come forth!" The figure of Christ stands with his arm raised, his mouth still open. Lazarus is coming out of the tomb, still wrapped in his burial clothes. Interestingly, the light does not shine on Christ, or even on Lazarus, as one might expect, but on the shocked faces of the observers. The art, then, focuses on the biblical story, but the artist illuminates the reaction of the people as if to say, what do you believe about this miracle worker? What is your faith response? The faith response seems to be the central theme of the work. Rembrandt obviously reflected deeply on the passage and perhaps wished to show his own identification with the observers—his own involvement with this biblical account.

Other artists in the seventeenth century also subordinated their art to theological themes. A good example is Jacob van Ruisdael (1628/29–1682), a contemporary of Rembrandt. His *Three Trees in a Mountainous Landscape with a River* (fig. 17) at first glance appears to be a straightforward landscape such as one might see from a particular location. And indeed Ruisdael may well have used motifs from a real setting. But a closer look betrays the larger purpose of the work. First of all, one is struck by the contrast between the light shining on the middle tree and the brokenness of that tree. Looking further one sees additional light in the sky in spite of the lengthening shadows throughout the painting. A few figures can be seen taking their sheep in for the night, returning from their labors as Psalm 104 puts it, but they are not the centerpiece; one has to look carefully to see them. The house on the left, which at first glance looked solid and comfortable, is actually falling into ruins. What is the meaning of this disarray? John Walford believes that Ruisdael had a theological message in mind. The artist wished to convey that though the sun is shining and there is beauty and meaning in the scene, there is also brokenness. Taking his cue from Ecclesiastes, which was a frequent subject of preachers of that time, Ruisdael interpreted "vanity" as "brokenness." One can enjoy life and savor its gifts, but note that the end of it is death. Still, light shines in the sky and especially on this central tree. Why? Light symbolizes hope and life, and here its focus on the tree recalls the one who died on the tree for us (indeed, the painting contains three trees, just as there were three crosses). One can therefore have hope in spite of the lengthening shadows.[13]

The rich landscapes of this period, the ordered domestic interiors, and especially the plain church interiors have all been attributed to Calvinist influence, and in general that may be the case.[14] But such developments may also be thought of as a continuation of an impulse for reform and simplicity that, as noted earlier, predated the Reformation—groups such as the Brethren of the Common Life, who fashioned a cultural style and space that resonated with the views the Reformers later articulated.

From a more positive perspective, this impulse toward order and simplicity can be seen as part of a literal and cognitive imagination that was developing in Protestant Europe, which would become evident in the mathematically based world picture of René Descartes and even in the chorales of Bach. It is especially represented in the Puritan stream of Christianity that settled in America. There are exceptions to this story in Europe, which we cannot focus on here. For example, the Anglican tradition in Britain (and later in America), which after the Restoration of the Monarch in 1660 prevailed over the Puritans, remained more open to the visual traditions of the medieval church and thus continued to give the visual a role in worship and devotional life. This openness led to the work of the nineteenth-century Pre-Raphaelites (so called for their desire to return to medieval religious practices and values). But in this brief account we follow the tradition of Calvin and the Puritans to the New World.

Based on evidence from the seventeenth century, it is clear that visual arts were practiced by Christians, and at a very high artistic level. But neither of the paintings just examined were made for worship or for a particular religious or devotional use, even though they do portray a powerful Christian view of the world. This restriction of art to the private realm, so to speak, did not deter Protestants from becoming artists. Indeed, seventeenth-century Dutch art represented a golden age of art in that country, and most of those artists were Christians, or at least were influenced by a reformed view of the world. Further, six of the twenty-four original members of the French Academy of Painting and Sculpture (founded in 1648) were Huguenots (French Reformed Protestants), which is interesting in light of the fact that Protestants made up only 5 or 6 percent of the total French population at that time.[15] But still, deep-seated attitudes continued to keep visual art from having any permanent alliance with worship.

This did not mean, however, that Christians were estranged from the world of art. After all, the primary purpose behind the founding of the French Academy, called the Royal Academy, which contained a high percentage of Protestant Christians (and certainly many Catholics), was to seek higher standards for art. To accomplish this, the members established a hierarchy of genres that they felt were important for artists to portray. These genres would serve as categories for regular exhibitions.[16] At the highest level was history painting, which held up before viewers the great events of history to show the ideal of heroic behavior. Allied with this genre were mythological subjects, which were also supposed to encourage proper morality and a life of decorum. Next came portrait painting. This too, depending on the social level of the subject, held up a noble ideal before the viewer. The category "fêtes gallantes" (gallant festivals) added later, was eventually broadened to include "pastoral" or common scenes, often with moral overtones. Painting, in other words, even if it did not have a specifically religious purpose, still played a moral role in society. People who carefully studied the best of these works would become better people, in part by enlarging their aesthetic and intellectual capacities. And all artists, whether Christian or not, gave their support to this general perspective on visual art. As we examine the modern period, we will want to inquire into the fate of such a hierarchy of genres.

The Visual Arts in America

The Puritans got their name in part from their desire to purify the church by returning to the simplicity of the truth of Scripture. William Ames, who had perhaps the greatest influence on the early Puritans, sought the "marrow of divinity" in what he called the plain style of teaching and preaching the Scriptures. These views influenced the architectural style of Puritan churches, which were called simply "meeting houses," and pointedly excluded anything in those spaces that would distract from the plain preaching of Scripture. The space and all decorations was subordinated to the central focus of worship: the preaching of the Word.

This tradition developed a unique profile in its new setting in America. On the one hand, it continued to focus on the inward and verbal dimensions of spirituality. But on the other hand, it focused on a creativity that looked for ways to build a community based on God's Word. For these and other reasons, there was little visual art during the seventeenth century, only the beginning of a tradition of portraiture, though things began to change after 1700.

Browsing through the Museum of Fine Arts in Boston, one is impressed with the portraiture, landscapes, and domestic interiors of the subsequent centuries, not unlike the Dutch art of the seventeenth century (of which such art might be said to be a cousin). But very little hints at the Christian story or the worship or devotional life of the church. The first references to Christianity in nineteenth-century art seem to be Scripture references written over landscape scenes. Unlike the early periods of Christian history, art was seen as having little or no particular theological content; it certainly had no relationship to the worshiping life of the church. This clearly had something to do with the thoroughly personal patterns of worship and spirituality that had developed by this time—and that had been especially encouraged in the pietist movements of the Old World and the revivals in the New.

Jonathan Edwards, for example, could paint powerful word pictures in his preaching, and he could, like Calvin, wax eloquent on the beauty of creation as God's means of bringing glory to himself. And yet when it came to the imagination and creativity, he saw only the activity of Satan:

> The imagination or fancy seems to be that wherein are formed all those delusions of Satan, which those are carried away with who are under the influence of false religion and counterfeit graces and affections. Here is the devil's grand lurking place, the very nest of foul and delusive spirits.[17]

At the same time, this inward and personal focus accommodated a literal imagination that consistently sought the distilled truth free of all imaginative decoration. This is interesting, for there is certainly no inherent reason why an inward spiritual focus could not come to expression in a richly elaborated visual culture. But in America, the developing worldview sought a clear and plain method for everything from the interpretation of Scripture to the running of revivals. By the end of the nineteenth century, a church was more likely to contain a chart outlining the ages of salvation history than a print or painting. Only in the form of a chart could the order of the world be made clear in Christian terms.

But a second influence of this way of thinking about the world was reflected particularly in American attitudes toward history: God wanted to do something new on this continent. Puritans in Plymouth believed that they were founding a city on a hill and that the eyes of all the world would be upon them. As a result, the focus of the "story" of America, for certain groups of Puritans, was on the future rather than the past. The past was over, and a bright future was opening up before them.[18] This predisposition was furthered by the romantic ideal of the artist as a seer into the future who was inspired by God (or the gods!). Americans, especially of the more conservative variety, despised developmentalism, that is, the idea that history was developing in a particular direction out of fixed traditions. They believed instead that history consists of inter-

Fig. 18. *The Blessing,* E. G. Dunnel. This item is reproduced by permission of The Huntington Library, San Marino, California.

mittent bursts of creativity.[19] This may help to account for the fact that evangelicals often think of their likeness to God in terms of absolute creativity—an idea that, we will note in the next chapter, has no support in Scripture.

This impulse to create a new world and reject the past may have had something to do with the iconoclastic temperament referred to earlier. In some cases, Robert Crawford has argued recently, iconoclasm has not only destroyed art but has actually fueled an art that focuses on what is new. He argues that this is particularly evident in the poetry of Byron and the early (more American) poetry of T. S. Eliot. Iconoclasm may be, he concludes, "an important impulse within the modern creative process."[20] This impulse seems particularly evident in the development of modern art.

Art in America, therefore, when it developed its own tradition in the nineteenth century, celebrated the making of what was completely new, something that would allow one to imagine a new future unhampered by the mistakes of the past. Interestingly, in the twentieth century, this "tradition of the new," as Robert Hughes has called it,[21] became the dominant tradition not only of American art but, since Impressionism at least, of all modern art. This view is connected with the tradition of the avant garde—that is, only the artist who has been liberated from all tradition and is in touch with the future and creating that future can be trusted as the source of guidance. Similarly, American Christians, caught up in the "new birth" that the revivals stimulated, consistently yearned for the purity of a reborn nature over against what they saw as a corrupt past.

By the nineteenth century, American Christians were developing their own visual culture. Early in that century, the American Tract Society followed its European counterparts and began to put illustrations on its tracts—though it was a controversial move. Would such illustrations detract from the message? Would they trivialize the gospel? Such popular art, when it did have religious connotations, served the ideal of a personal and inward spirituality. Notice the print *The Blessing* (fig. 18) by engraver E. G. Dunnel (fl. 1847), which celebrates a Christian home and its family prayer before a meal. This print is typical of many that became popular in the nineteenth century. Under the influence of Horace Bushnell's famous work, *Christian Nurture* (1847), a stream of piety developed that sought to use wholesome images of faith and comfort to encourage Christian nurture, especially of children. This popular art developed a kind of aesthetic of reassurance that continued in the twentieth century in the extremely popular work of Warner Sallman (1892–1968). More recently, Thomas Kinkade (1958–) has created an extremely popular line of prints that similarly celebrate images of security. While these images have played an important role in the lives of many, sustaining them and providing comfort, they have done little either to connect with Christian traditions of the past or to begin a creative movement that could be sustained.[22] An evaluation of this type of work is perhaps best illustrated by the life of Dunnel. Not long after he finished this print, he gave up art altogether and entered the ministry!

Christians and the Arts in the Twentieth Century: Is a Renaissance Under Way?

In a later chapter, I lay out the challenges of the contemporary situation in the visual arts in more detail. Here we look in particular at the growing Christian interaction with the visual arts in the twentieth century. I have described some of the handicaps that Protestants work with, some of which stretch back to the Reformation. But in the early twentieth century, the situation, if anything, became worse. Following the liberal-fundamentalist debates in the first decades of the century, evangelicals withdrew from involvement in the larger culture, fearing that such involvement might compromise their Christian witness. They separated themselves from modern culture and shaped institutions that more nearly reflected their view of purity and discipleship. Recent scholarship has corrected a previous tendency to overstate this isolation by pointing out that many evangelicals did in fact make use of elements of modern culture, especially modern youth culture and its media, to reach out to their neighbors with the gospel. While such steps led to innovations in evangelism (and thus indirectly in worship—one thinks of the choruses of the Youth for Christ rallies or the praise choruses today), they did not initially lead to a serious interaction with the arts. But this is changing.

Three streams have had an influence on developing Protestant and evangelical attitudes toward the visual arts. The first would surely be the influence of Paul Tillich (1886–1965), who gave the arts, and the visual arts in particular, an important place in his theology. Many modern theologians have made positive reference to the arts in their work—one thinks for example of Karl Barth's extended description of the music of Mozart—but Tillich was unique in giving a theological depth of meaning to the arts as an important part of his theological method.

Tillich's interest in art began in the trenches of World War I. During this period, he notes, art became his hobby, but it was also an antidote to the ugliness of war.[23] Shortly after the war, he began teaching at the University of Berlin, across the street from the museum of contemporary art, where battles were being fought between the modernists and those who would later become the supporters of Adolf Hitler. German expressionism became a favorite style of Tillich. Later he came to America, where he taught at Union Seminary in New York and later at the University of Chicago.

We have spent some time tracing the development of Christian attitudes toward the arts and cultures. One of the results of these developments is that religion and spirituality have progressively come to be identified with the inner world. Meanwhile, an increasingly secularized culture has accepted as a given that religion has little to do with everyday life in the world. It is precisely this split between the secular and the sacred that Tillich so effectively addressed.

Tillich's most important contribution was showing the intrinsic relationship between religion and art. He understood art as an "encounter of man with his world, in which the whole man in all dimensions of his being is involved."[24] He felt this encounter was similar to a religious experience, as both "create symbols and require participation in these symbols in order to be understood."[25] As he often put it, religion is the substance of culture, and culture is the form of religion. This is because religion is fundamentally the experience of the ultimate meaning of life rooted in the ground of being (or God), and all creative art is based in some way on an encounter with this reality.[26] Artists reflect this connection through their use of symbols. Symbols, in contrast to signs, participate in the power of what they represent; they "open up dimensions of reality which cannot be grasped any other way."[27] Certain styles of art, therefore, are able to represent to the viewer the depths of reality in ways that ordinary experience cannot.

It is clear from these comments that Tillich's views were determined by his fundamental view of reality, which continued a long tradition of German idealism—that reality is grounded in a spirit or mind. His insistence on the relationship between religious faith and the experience of art has been suggestive and influential for many people who have considered the integration of religion and the arts. But while his views were helpful in describing a possible integration between the practices and feelings of religion and art, they were less helpful in integrating theology—that is, particular views about God and the world—and the arts. Though his discussion of symbolism has been widely influential, Tillich was unable to provide any criteria by which the adequacy of symbols can be judged. The participation of symbols in reality, as Anthony Thistleton has pointed out, speaks to their power, but it does not address their truth.[28] Further, Tillich's view of symbolism reduces all language about God to a symbolism that provides no way of making literal statements about God and particularly about his activity in creation and redemption.

In the end, Tillich's categories proved too blunt and nondiscriminating to provide much help in understanding language, metaphor, and artistic development. But he deserves credit for raising a series of important questions about culture, religion, and their relationship. In probably the last address Tillich gave on theology and art, he seemed to sense the bewildering new world that was developing and the changes this world would necessitate: "We have a whole cemetery of dead categories. And this certainly is a situation which makes us dizzy: A kind of metaphysical dizziness grasps us. Yet we must encounter it; we cannot avoid it by looking back to the wonderful fixed world of the years before 1900 in which everything felt familiar. . . . This world no longer exists."[29]

In America, Tillich is important for the influence he exerted on a wide variety of Christians since World War II, indeed, for developing a new discussion around religion and the arts. In many respects, up to the last decade the major voices speaking about theology and art were those who knew or studied with him: John and Jane Dillenberger at the Graduate Theological Union in Berkeley, Tom Driver and those associated with the Association of Religion and the Arts in New York, and Nathan Scott, who developed the prestigious theology and literature program at the University of Chicago.

A second stream of influence, especially in the evangelical wing of the church in America, is a group of Reformed thinkers who work in the tradition begun by John Calvin and developed in the nineteenth century by Abraham Kuyper and in the last century by Herman Dooyeweerd and who have begun to take the arts and culture seriously. Most prominent among these were Francis Schaeffer and Hans Rookmaaker. During the 1960s and 1970s, through their lecturing and writing, these thinkers did more than any other single influence to raise issues related to Christianity and culture among conservative Christians.[30] As a result of the split between the inner spiritual world and the outer more secular world, Christians in the twentieth century often retreated from any direct involvement in the larger world of culture, as we have noted. These thinkers directly addressed this issue of cultural involvement.

Francis Schaeffer (1912–1984) was more a prophet and evangelist than a scholar, and in this role he did much to awaken the evangelical movement to its cultural responsibilities. After his graduation from seminary, he was sent as a missionary to Switzerland, where in 1955 he founded L'Abri, a Christian study center that now has branches in England, Holland, and the United States. He was known for confronting existentialist and nihilistic worldviews with the implications of their thinking—taking the roof off these worldviews, as he put it (showing the final and fatal implications of these views)—so that adherents would be open to hear the gospel in a new way. He used developments in art and culture to illustrate the spiritual quest of twentieth-century people and the philosophical nihilism that was often reflected there. For his cultural analysis he was dependent on Rookmaaker's interpretation of history, especially, of modern art and the implications these developments had for evangelism.

Hans Rookmaaker (d. 1977) was a respected professor of art history at the Free University of Amsterdam (Holland). Rookmaaker had become a Christian by reading Dutch philosopher Herman Dooyeweerd while in an internment camp during World War II. His thinking, thus, was deeply influenced by the neo-Reformed perspective of Dooyeweerd. Unlike Schaeffer, as a scholar and professor, Rookmaaker's influence was exercised more through his students and his writing than his popular lectures. His *Modern Art and the Death of a Culture* (1971) still stands as a landmark attempt to describe the puzzling developments in modern art in terms of a Christian worldview. But he also encouraged the development of Christian art groups in England and America as well as his native Holland.

While not formally aligned with Schaeffer and Rookmaaker, other scholars have subsequently helped to shape this reformed outlook on art and culture, most notably Nicholas Wolterstorff (first at Calvin College and now at Yale University) and Calvin Seerveld (at the Institute of Christian Studies in Toronto).

Together they have shaped a view of culture that emphasizes the purposes of God in creation and sees art as a part of the obedient response of believers to the call of God. For these thinkers, as I will note in a later chapter, good art in general and Christian art in particular is nothing special; it is simply "sound, healthy, good art. It is art that is in line with the God-given structures of art, one which has a loving and free view on reality, one which is good and true."[31]

A final stream of influence is the impact of renewed conversation on the part of Protestants with the major traditions of the church, in particular the Roman Catholic and, to a lesser extent, the Orthodox traditions. A problem we have noted in Protestant attitudes toward the visual arts has been the historical isolation of Protestants. Since the Reformation they found themselves cut off from the rich artistic traditions of the church. Since Vatican II, however, which ended in 1965, there has been a renewed openness and conversation between the Catholic and Protestant branches of the church. In particular, Catholic notions of spirituality and the traditions of spiritual practices that date back to the Middle Ages have increasingly influenced Protestants, especially their understanding of spirituality and worship. These influences represent, for the most part, not an encouragement to appreciate art but an attempt to recover a deeper tradition of spirituality. It turns out, however, that this tradition is firmly attached to various artistic media—icons, altarpieces, and so on. Through retreats and conferences that have featured these traditional practices, many Protestants have begun to see the importance of visual dimensions of faith and practice. As a result, they are increasingly open to learning from the historical developments surveyed in this and the previous chapter.

The Catholic tradition was able to exert a fresh influence on the Protestant Church in part because of its own renewal in the twentieth century, a renewal that led up to and followed the Vatican council in the 1960s. A significant Catholic revival in France, which took place around the turn of the nineteenth century, had a profound impact on the culture of that country and beyond. A small group of writers and scholars, such as J. K. Huysmans, Leon Bloy, and Jacques and Raissa Maritain, began to express a radical Christian faith that was characterized by deep lifestyle changes and formation of Christian community and that attracted a wide following. Their efforts influenced a generation of artists and writers in a way that revivified the arts in the Catholic Church—which like other churches had long been an opponent of modern styles of art. Paul Claudel, George Bernanos, François Mauriac, and others were a product of this movement—some such as Graham Greene were indirect fruits of the revival. In the visual arts, Georges Rouault was representative of this group.[32] Meanwhile, other Catholic writers working in aesthetics, Hans von Balthasar and Patrick Sherry, have attracted a wide following among Protestants as well as Catholics. Again, I will comment further on these below.

It is obviously not my intent to write a complete history of the interaction between theology and the visual arts in the last fifty years. But it is clear that the influences described have resulted in a sea change in attitudes toward the visual arts. Moreover, all those involved in this renewal were, more than likely, influenced by one or more of these three streams.[33] One way of tracking this transformation is to note the literature on Christianity or theology and the arts. Up until roughly 1960, about the only book available for Christians was an exhaustive collection of materials by Cynthia Pearl Maus, *Christ and the Fine Arts*.[34] This anthology of pictures, poetry, and even music centered on the life of Christ but did not provide critical or historical reflection. The 1960s, however, experienced a virtual explosion of books exploring this topic, many of them thoughtful and theologically sophisticated. Finley Eversole and Nathan Scott brought together important essays on various aspects of the relationship between theology and the arts.[35] Roger Hazelton and Donald Whittle wrote important books;[36] G. Wilson Knight wrote about a "Christian Renaissance";[37] and Gerhardus Van der Leeuw, in a book that continues to be influential, described the way the earthly material world is capable of bearing the divine reality, as a witness to the incarnation.[38] In addition to Rookmaaker and Schaeffer, other evangelicals also began writing on the topic during this time. Among these were Derek Kidner, Calvin Seerveld, and Bruce Lockerbie.[39]

These influences merged in subsequent decades with other more general cultural developments. Evangelicals in the twentieth century typically made use of modern media, especially in relation to evangelism and missions. This became especially evident with the revivals in California during the late 1960s and early 1970s that fostered the Jesus People. These converts, when they joined the church, brought with them their love for popular culture, both in its musical and visual dimensions, for this was the first generation raised on a steady diet of TV. Not all churches were open to these long-haired, guitar-toting Christians, but those that were found their worship life profoundly changed, and they continue to push the edges in innovations in music and worship and, to a lesser extent, the visual arts.

Initially, the influence of these highly creative believers was limited to the so-called new paradigm churches that welcomed them—Calvary Chapels and later the Vineyard Movement. But by the 1980s and 1990s their influence and the influence of the praise choruses they wrote and sang had made their way into the broader pop culture. Their music and penchant for the visual gradually began to make their way into mainline churches, resulting frequently in tensions known as worship wars. But these developments inevitably created a new openness to innovation both in the musical and the visual arenas.

By the end of the twentieth century, a proliferation of people and groups were paying attention to the arts and reflecting on their use in worship and their theological significance. Early in the 1990s, the Association of Theological Schools sponsored a series of consultations on the use of the arts in theological education.[40] In Cambridge, a multiyear project entitled "Theology through the Arts" recently concluded its first phase. Directed by Jeremy Begbie of Ridley College, this program of research and performance culminated in an impressive arts festival during September of 2000 in Cambridge. Christians in the Visual Arts (CIVA), an international network of Christians in the arts (though focused largely in the United States and Canada), has already sponsored an impressive list of conferences and publications that promise to raise the level of both discussion and artistic quality. *Image: A Journal of the Arts and Religion* also came to prominence during this time, serving as a thoughtful and prestigious forum for conversations about faith and art.

Interestingly, these initiatives are by no means limited to Protestants or to evangelicals; indeed, in all three cases they are clearly ecumenical in the best sense of the word—that is, they include voices from all sections of the church. All of them, moreover, exhibit in various ways the impact of the three influences described above and their efforts to reclaim a lost heritage of Christianity and the arts. Not only are Protestants reconnecting with a part of their heritage that was lost, but they are frequently doing so in partnership with believers from other parts of the church universal.

But while there is much for which we can be thankful, there is still much that remains to be done. The fact that much controversy attends the use of arts in worship, that artists in Christian communities continue to be marginalized, and that Christians still express confusion regarding their engagement with the arts indicates unfinished business. Part of this work is clearly a recovery of the historical lineage reviewed in this and the previous chapter. But a further arguably more important part of our work is the recovery of a biblical warrant for our engagement with this dimension of culture. It is to this work that we now turn.

art and
the biblical drama

3

In addition to reviewing historical materials, we must reflect on the resources that Scripture provides in order to develop a Christian perspective on the arts. From the point of view of Scripture, were the Reformers correct in believing that the Christian tradition had lost its way with respect to the visual arts? And what guidance can Scripture give us today regarding a biblical aesthetic? As many commentators have pointed out, the biblical material, on first glance at least, appears to provide little help in developing a positive view of art and aesthetics. C. S. Lewis is typical of many when he says that the New Testament seems to make the salvation of human souls the real business of life. It would appear that whatever conflicts with this central concern must clearly be secondary. He concludes: "On the whole, the New Testament seemed, if not hostile, yet unmistakably cold to culture. I think we can still believe culture to be innocent after we have read the New Testament; I cannot see that we are encouraged to think it important."[1] Similarly, Derek Kidner begins his study *The Christian and the Arts* by admitting that "the whole weight of the biblical emphasis is on the dangers, not the advantages, of the leisured conditions in which the arts flourish and in which the Greeks sought to cultivate the good life."[2]

But a deeper examination of biblical materials shows that there is an important biblical pathway to thinking about the arts. Kidner's recognition that the Bible does not support the Greek view of "leisured culture," still so important in some elite circles today, is an important starting point. Biblical materials may not support some views of art that are current today and have their roots in the Greek tradition—certain ways of thinking about avant garde art, for example. But this is by no means the only way of thinking about art, and indeed, according to Scripture, this attitude toward the arts may be a perversion of the Creator's intention. Part of the problem is the modern habit of dividing up life into tidy little areas—art, morality, or business—each with its own subculture and discourse. In the biblical view, by contrast, life is viewed holistically—aesthetic and ethical (even economic) questions are constantly interrelated. Moreover, none of these important areas can be properly considered apart from their connection to the Creator and his purposes for the earth and its people. In other words, artistic issues are, according to the biblical perspective, profoundly theological from beginning to end.

Biblical Framework

Biblical Language for Beauty and Goodness

What do we mean when we say that something is "beautiful"? This word is used in so many contexts today that for many people it has no clear meaning—one would be as likely to hear it after a good basketball shot as in an art museum. This is partly because its meaning has changed over time. In classical Greece, Plato taught that beauty is a property of particular objects that are balanced, ordered, and possess internal unity. Beauty, in other words, was an objective property of objects in the world. Since John Locke focused on the way we experience reality through the senses, however, beauty has come to refer to the experience of an observer. Beauty in the modern period, while obviously not void of all objective reference, has acquired a highly subjective coloring. Even when it is used in connection with a fine painting, therefore, the word *beautiful* refers to a particular experience of aesthetic contemplation. Moreover, the encounter with beauty is often a unique and personal experience that is separate from the rest of life, something we experience in the quiet of museums and concert halls.

A useful place to begin, then, is to examine biblical language for art and beauty and compare it with the way these words are used today. We will examine briefly some of the language the Old Testament—and more briefly the New Testament—uses for the aesthetic dimension of life.[3] Part of the modern problem is that the Hebrews had no special language for art and beauty, precisely because beauty was not something that occupied a separate part of their lives. In one sense, it was "nothing special." Often objects of beauty simply accompanied or adorned ordinary parts of life and therefore would likely be dismissed today as merely "decorative." Beauty was nothing special because at its best it was meant to be a reflection of the ordered meaning of God's good creation. Often references to what we would call beauty are best translated merely as what is "fitting" or simply "good." To illustrate this, let us look briefly at the seven word groups in Hebrew that refer to what is lovely or to the enjoyment of these things.[4]

1. The Hebrew word *tsebi* appears eighteen times in the Old Testament and means either "beauty" or "honor." It also refers to the gazelle.[5] In this sense, beauty is a quality that merits the admiration of others, as when David cries out upon hearing of the death of Jonathan and Saul, "Your beauty is slain upon the high places" (2 Sam. 1:19, in this chapter, my translation unless noted). Often it is used of nations, either characterizing that of which one can properly boast (but which God can eliminate by judgment), as in references to "Babylon, the glory *[tsebi]* of kingdoms" (Isa. 13:19), or referring to the goodness of God's Promised Land, especially Jerusalem itself: "I thought how I would give you . . . a heritage more beautiful than all the nations" (Jer. 3:19). In Isaiah 28:5, the reference is to the Lord himself, who will be a "crown of beauty." Here, therefore, beauty is that which naturally sparks admiration but which can also be the cause of undue pride and thus merit God's righteous judgment. But it can also refer to the final kingdom, the perfection of Canaan's own goodness, Zion, or the New Jerusalem (Isa. 4:5). The meanings can overlap with moral judgments and frequently have explicit connections with the narrative that describes the future promises of God—which I examine below.

2. A closely related word group contains words related to the verb *hadar,* meaning "to honor or glorify" and appearing thirty-seven times in all forms. This too is that character of honor freely acknowledged with respect to God or the king. When used in reference to God, this character of glory appears as the visible expression of his power and holiness—a kind of perceived holiness (1 Chron. 16:27). He is clothed with it (Ps. 104:1) and can clothe others with this quality: "You have . . . crowned [them] with glory and honor *[kabod wehadar]*" (Ps. 8:5). It can also refer to the splendor of "holy adornment" (Ps. 29:2)—probably a reference to the splendor of the dress of those leading worship. A parallel reference in Psalm 96:9 goes on to say, "tremble before him, all the earth," indicating that this beauty was to inspire a proper sense of God's holiness and was not meant to be only a visual spectacle. Again there is a frequent connection between what is lovely and what is good, even holy.

3. These connections also feature in meanings of *pa'ar,* a verb used thirteen times: "to glorify," "to crown," or "to beautify." The sense of the word implies making something into an object of adoration or praise, or to give it a place of honor. The king was praised for seeking "to glorify" God's house (Ezra 7:27), though people can improperly seek this for themselves by "vaunting themselves" (Judg. 7:2 RSV). Once again God promises to glorify his people, as in this striking promise to Israel: "You are my servant in whom I will be beautiful" (Isa. 49:3). Clearly this implies a visual splendor but one that includes a moral dimension. The related noun *tip'arah* appears forty-nine times and means "ornament," "splendor," or "glory." The word is often used of that which has an outward splendor, such as Aaron's robes (Exod. 28:2), but it can also extend to a full splendor, as in Ezekiel's moving allegory of Israel's future when God will "put . . . a beautiful crown on your head" (Ezek. 16:12). It is used of the pomp and

(presumably visual) display of the king in Esther 1:4, and it is even used in reference to something of which one might be proud, such as an old man's gray head (Prov. 16:31), or the beauty with which a bridegroom decks himself (Isa. 61:10), even God's name (1 Chron. 29:13). Finally, this word will characterize the Lord in the last day (Isa. 28:5) as well as his people: "I will put salvation in Zion for Israel my beauty" (Isa. 46:13c).

4. Words associated with the verb *hamad,* meaning "to desire" or "to delight in," reflect the interconnection of beauty and desire, for they often refer to a desire that sparks the intention of obtaining the object for oneself. The root refers to what is pleasant in such a way that it drives one to take action. This can have a positive sense, as with the trees in the Garden that God created for delight (Gen. 2:9), or the delight one feels for one's beloved (Song of Sol. 2:3), or the mount God desires for his dwelling (Ps. 68:16). But it can also refer to the desire for what is forbidden, as when Achan "coveted in gold" (Josh. 7:21), or when the rich coveted the fields of the poor (Micah 2:2). Such a desire is summed up in the last commandment, which uses this word: "You shall not desire—see as attractive—anything that is your neighbor's" (Exod. 20:17). The nouns derived from this word usually refer to what is pleasant or lovely and therefore precious, such as the land God gave to Israel, or stones or precious vessels—what we might call "valuables" (2 Chron. 32:27). While this beauty may be dangerous, it is clear that God does not despise it, for on the day of the Lord he promises to shake nations as one would shake a fruit tree, "so that the treasures *[hemdat]* of all nations will come into it. And it will fill this house with glory says the Lord of Hosts. This silver is mine and the gold is mine, says the Lord of Hosts" (Hag. 2:7–8, see the allusion to this verse in Rev. 21:24).

5. Words associated with the verb *yafah,* "to be fair or beautiful," appear over sixty times in all their forms. These words ordinarily refer to the outward beauty of a person or, less frequently, an object. It is the frequent descriptor of the beloved in Song of Solomon, and it is used to describe Sarah (Gen. 12:11), Joseph (39:6), and Esther (Esther 2:7). Israel is called lovely because of God's goodness to her, as in Jeremiah 11:16: "a green olive tree, fair with good fruit." This beauty is dangerous only when it becomes a source of pride, as in Ezekiel 16. In this moving passage, under God's loving care, Israel had become famous for her beauty (vv. 12–14), but then she trusted in her beauty (v. 15) so that she offered herself to those who passed by in harlotry (v. 25). Finally, this beauty again describes God's very presence in Zion: "Out of Zion, the perfect beauty, God shines forth" (Ps. 50:2), as well as God's people in the last days (Zech. 9:17). Especially interesting is the frequent appearance of this word group in the wisdom literature, where it indicates the highest perfection that God's good creation can reach. He has made everything beautiful in its time, says the preacher (Eccles. 3:11). All of this is lovely to enjoy, but taken out of context it becomes ugly: "Like a gold ring in a swine's snout is a beautiful woman with no discretion" (Prov. 11:22).[6]

6. What is "fitting" is especially characteristic of the words associated with the verb *na'ah*. The word can mean the physically attractive (as in Song of Sol. 1:1), but more often it means what is pleasing, in the sense of what is suitable to a given situation or context. Praise "suits" the righteous (Ps. 33:1), holiness "belongs" in God's house (Ps. 93:5; cf. NEB, "holiness is the beauty of thy house"), and the feet of the evangelist are "lovely" (Isa. 52:7). By contrast, lovely words are decidedly out of place in the mouth of a fool (Prov. 17:7), nor are a fine house or honor "suited" to a fool (Prov. 19:10; 26:1).

7. Words associated with *na'em* refer to what is pleasant or lovely in a general sense. It refers to the Promised Land (Gen. 49:15), words (Prov. 16:24), the places the psalmist is able to enjoy (Ps. 16:6), even bread eaten in secret (Prov. 9:17). When used in reference to a person, it refers more often to one's character than one's appearance: Jonathan was "good" to David (2 Sam. 1:26), while David was a "lovely" (talented?) psalmist (23:1). Brothers dwelling together in unity are described this way (Ps. 133:1), and even a rebuke for the wicked is pleasant in this sense (Prov. 24:25). This moral dimension is clear when God's presence is described in this way: "May the beauty of the Lord dwell among us" (Ps. 90:17), and when the believer looks forward to a fullness of joy and pleasures *[ne'imot]* when he or she enjoys the presence of God (Ps. 16:11).

Turning to the New Testament, the only reference to beauty in the narrow sense appears in Philippians 4:8: "Whatever is pleasing [or lovely]," from the Greek *prosphilēs* (the only appearance of this word in the New Testament). If anything, words that might indicate physical beauty are more strictly pressed into moral (and even theological) duty. The word for good *(kalos)*, for example, does not appear to be used of beauty in the narrow sense, though it can easily have this connotation (and does in other Greek literature). It is used of good fruit (Matt. 3:10), or a good deed (Matt. 13:24); Christ is the Good Shepherd (John 10:11, 14), and every creature of God is good and to be received (1 Tim. 4:4). But too much can easily be made of the absence of references to beauty in the New Testament. After all, for the writers of the New Testament, the Hebrew Scriptures constituted the authoritative Word from God. They did not find it necessary to repeat all the currents of Old Testament thought, though they surely embraced them.

From one point of view, the biblical language for beauty is unremarkable. Indeed, it shares some of its usage, even its vocabulary, with other Near Eastern cultures. And many languages today would express a similar holistic perspective. But biblical language is unique in grounding its holism in the presence and activity of a living and active God and in a world embracing the purposes of this God. This brief review of language, then, suggests the following starting points for our biblical discussion of visual art.

Both Testaments support the view that beauty and goodness have theological grounding. As the apocryphal Wisdom 13:3 puts it: "God is the author of all beauty." The conviction runs throughout Scripture that God is the source of beauty; he can give it or he can take it away. The splendor of beauty, its attractiveness, is grounded in the fact that it is inherent both in God himself and, by extension, in the creation that he has made and that bears his mark (it is, by God's standards, "very good").

Precisely for this reason, in no sense is the created order despised, as in Greek philosophy, because of its materiality. Creaturely beauty is never despised as a lesser beauty—indeed, the same word is frequently used in reference to the creature and to God. Rather, the creation displays in its creaturely way, when it is doing what God made it to do, qualities and values that God himself possesses. This not only makes possible our enjoyment of the created world but, more importantly, allows it to be a theater in which God can properly carry out his work of drawing people to himself.

This affirmation of the created order adds an important dimension to the holism referred to above. Because God has made the world "very good" and continues to work out his purposes in it, all its values are ultimately—at least potentially—related to these purposes. They are created to move in a single direction, to work on a single grand project. It is in this sense that visual beauty, inward splendor (what we might call "character"), and even truth are, in biblical terms, interrelated. As Calvin Seerveld puts this, "Truth is the way that God does things," for as truth is not so much an abstract quality as in Greek philosophy but an embodied way of being and doing, so beauty is the outward aspect of God's work within creation, indeed, of his own being. Ultimately, the Bible insists, this way of being is related to God's own acting and speaking. And so, Seerveld notes, "To experience or declare what is true [and I would add, what is beautiful] gets one actively caught up in the fabric of protecting, strengthening [and] opening communion with the Almighty Holy One."[7] Note, then, how the interconnection of beauty and morality, grounded as it is in God's person and acts, suggests that these terms are ultimately religious at their cores.

Finally, we have seen that the "charm" or "attractiveness" of beauty is in an important sense eschatological. That is, these qualities point toward a future for the earth when the fullness of what we see in beauty will be fully seen and known. I will have more to say on this point below.

These elements all stand in contrast to much that passes for beauty in our modern (and postmodern) discussions. While we are likely to see beauty and goodness as projections of our personal and cultural values, biblical language connects these characteristics to God and grounds them in the created order and the community in which humans are called to live. Although today we are not likely to connect beauty with human character, the Bible insists that they both relate to common values that are grounded in God and his creation. For some people, beauty has achieved such an important place that, rather than pointing to a God-shaped future, it actually has become a kind of secular eschatology—it is what they live for. It is the closest that many come to experiencing what the Bible calls the beauty of holiness. But in biblical terms this language for the splendor of creation is rooted in a larger narrative, and so to fully understand beauty we need to have a firm grasp of this narrative.

According to the Bible, then, what is visually lovely and true reflects who God is and, consequently, all that he does. A discussion of the personal and trinitarian character of God follows in the next chapter, but here we reflect further on the action of God. If truth and beauty reflect the "way God does things," as Seerveld argues, then the very coherence of these acts is something that must be called lovely. If the notes (acts) of God are themselves lovely, the melody (the story) that these notes shape must be even lovelier. Reflecting even briefly on this coherence reveals how this can be so.

The creation itself, which is said to result from both God's word and his acts—which often cannot be separated—is frequently described in the biblical account as "good" (*tob*), and God himself saw that it was "very good" (Gen. 1:31). Clearly, this means among other things that it was visually lovely, but it also means that things worked together in a special way—the sun worked with the earth to create life, animals fit into natural processes, and the human creation had its special (though not central) role to play. But beyond this it was good in the sense that something could happen with it that would make its splendor more splendid! Or, sadly, something could happen to injure this coherence and destroy its beauty. Thus, a sense of drama, of vulnerability and uncertainty, was built into the order that God insisted was very good.

Therefore, goodness, even beauty, are not fixed qualities toward which we can aspire—as was the case with the Greek ideal of perfection and beauty. Rather, they have a contingent character so familiar to anyone who treasures roses or sunsets. They refer back to God and in this sense "glorify" God as they were meant to do. But note that all creation is beautiful because it praises (glorifies, exalts) God. If we limit the praise of God to what we consider beautiful, we are stuck again with the modern temptation to project our feelings and desires on to God. As other references to creation show, especially Psalm 104, creation's very continuing existence (and not simply its beauty) expresses this continuing praise of God. True, creation is filled with things that delight the eyes (Gen. 3:6). But as we have seen, this quality is ambiguous; beauty can be a motivation to praise the Creator, but it can also serve to distract the creatures from their true end (when it is separated from God's larger purposes).

This seduction, in fact, takes place when the temptor succeeds in getting Adam and Eve to view creation's splendor on its own terms, that is, without reference to its Creator (Gen. 2:9; 3:6). This temptation introduces the possibility of that fatal dichotomy between beauty and goodness—something that clearly was the result of that first sin. When Adam and Eve are drawn to the beauty of the tree outside the moral context in which it was given, they take the first fatal step toward making beauty into an idol. They fail to appreciate that the beauty that draws them is part and parcel of the Word of God that instructs them—"the tree of the knowledge of good and evil you shall not eat."

One cannot fully enjoy the former without the latter. With Adam and Eve's disobedience, the ecology of relationships, with God, each other, and the created order, is disturbed—with both moral and aesthetic consequences (3:15–19).

This disruption works its way out in the narrative of Genesis until it results in the initial judgment of God in the form of a flood and the (merciful) scattering of people in Genesis 10. While the calling of Abraham results in a promise of hope, fertility, and blessing in the Promised Land (which frequently in Deuteronomy is described as beautiful), Genesis ends with Joseph in a coffin, as death intrudes where God intended life.

In Exodus, however, God hears the cries of his people and comes down to show his glory in their deliverance from slavery and from the death meted out on their enemies. This deliverance itself becomes the object of Israel's praise throughout their history—it becomes one of those acts of deliverance that is described as righteous, and beautiful, for again these notions are cousins. In the song of Moses, God's people sing:

> Who is like you, O LORD, among the gods?
> Who is like you, majestic in holiness,
> awesome in splendor, doing wonders?
>
> Exodus 15:11 NRSV

When Moses ascends the mountain, there is smoke, thunder, lightning, earthquake. Again the power and holiness of God are displayed in a way that exhibits an outward visual display, powerful both in its dramatic and visual impact. Then in a splendid but often overlooked passage, Moses, Aaron, and all the elders went up, "and they saw the God of Israel. Under his feet there was something like a pavement of sapphire stone, like the very heaven for clearness." Then in a delightful aside the text notes, "They beheld God, and they ate and drank" (Exod. 24:10–11 NRSV). Here is an early reference to the connection between the presence of God and extraordinary visual display and splendor, something that will become important in the building of the temple and to the aesthetics of worship.

In the display of God's power, however, God is doing something. He is bringing his people out of slavery and into the land of promise. As we have seen, the land itself, and especially Jerusalem, are frequently called "good" and "lovely," not for their appearance alone but for what they come to mean in terms of God's presence and what he will do with these places. Israel, and its focus on Zion (the mountain in Jerusalem on which the temple is built), becomes the means by which the "goodness" of the original creation is again celebrated—Jerusalem is called "beautiful in elevation, . . . the joy of all the earth" (Ps. 48:2 NRSV). Frequently in the Book of Deuteronomy the land is called that "good" land, and Ezekiel calls it the most "glorious of all lands" (Ezek. 20:6). This clearly means that the land is fertile, but beyond that it is lovely both because it shares in the created splendor and because God is doing something with it that all the world will one day recognize and enjoy. The land becomes both the means and the object of God's promise. Again one might say that the events that brought Israel into (and out of) the land have their own "splendor." Their glory relates as much to God's purposeful actions as to any visible "goodness."

In one sense, Old Testament aesthetics comes to focus in the tabernacle and later the temple as the place where God's visual glory dwells. The first time God's Spirit comes upon anyone for some special task is when Bezalel and Oholiab are commissioned to devise artistic design and furnish the tabernacle. Bezalel seems to have been especially gifted as a craftsman; Oholiab was a kind of interior designer (see Exod. 31:1–11). The language here—knowledge, skill, wisdom—is clearly the language of the wisdom tradition. This tradition reflects those in Israel who were able to discern and put into practice the goodness and splendor of God's creation and who were responsible for much of what we call the wisdom literature (especially the Proverbs and much of Psalms). This first mention of people we would call artists or craftsmen (they would have been indistinguishable in Israel) is found, then, in the context of wisdom. But interestingly, such skill is also said to result from a particular gifting of God's Spirit ("I have filled [Bezalel] with divine spirit" [31:2 NRSV]). This is significant in light of the discussion of the Trinity in the next chapter, for it will become clear that the special work of the Spirit is to work within creation to shape the creature in a way that will glorify God. Here, then, is an early glimmer of the full work of God in redeeming creation.

Bezalel and Oholiab worked in areas of craft, construction, design, vestments, even incense—incorporating many senses and types of craft into the making of an appropriate space for worship. But note above all, as with the later design and construction of the temple, that God is intimately involved in both the design and construction. Of special interest is the use of representational sculpture in the form of cherubim, which was to be placed over the mercy seat (and probably reflects motifs common in Near Eastern art [Exod. 25:18–22]). All is specified in great detail, but the work is given over to those specially gifted (by God) for this task: preparing a space suitable for the worship of God. It was clearly important to God that this be a beautiful space because, as he says, "There I will meet with you" (25:22 NRSV). Indeed, he goes further, specifying that from between the cherubim and from above the altar, "I will deliver to you all my commands for the Israelites."

The tabernacle and the temple were central both to the worship life and to the identity of the people of Israel. The distress of the exile was caused in large part by having to leave the land behind and by being separated from the temple, for this was the place where God promised that his name would dwell. God told Solomon, "I have consecrated this house that you have built, and put my name there forever; my eyes and my heart will be there for all time" (1 Kings

9:3 NRSV). But God's presence was also connected with Solomon's responsibility to God and God's people, for God goes on to say that if Solomon walks before God with integrity, as David did before him, God would establish his throne forever. To underline this promise God's glory entered the temple as a cloud at the dedication (1 Kings 8:10). This visual event signified that God's holiness was there—the visual and the moral were intertwined. The worship life of Israel, therefore, revolved around the temple worship and the regular feasts associated with that worship. The great worship book of Israel, the Psalms, is filled with expressions of the splendor of God and the temple and the joy of meeting God in that place. Going up to the temple was a visual metaphor for going up to God (see Psalm 122).

The word study revealed that often the prophets referred to the beauty both of Jerusalem and God's people. But they also frequently used similar words for the day of the Lord that they saw in the future. Often, as noted, biblical references to beauty, and goodness for that matter, have a future reference, for it is clear that the disruption caused by sin has influenced our experience of beauty, even as it has disrupted our sense of the good. Accordingly, in the prophets the absence of beauty is sometimes associated with the oppression of the poor (Amos 2). But the prophets believed that events in history were moving toward an earthshaking settlement that would involve a radical reordering of things. The prophets, therefore, offered symbols "adequate to the horror and massiveness of an experience which evokes numbness and requires denial."[8] This promised deliverance (and judgment) was referred to as the day of the Lord. Though Amos described this day as darkness and gloom rather than brightness and light (Amos 5:20), it can also be described in terms of great beauty. In that day Israel will be a "crown of beauty in the hand of the LORD" (Isa. 62:3 NRSV). Not only will the land and its people be fair, but the whole will be painted together as delightful, for "your God will be your glory" (Isa. 60:19 NRSV).

Images of glory concentrate themselves around a few key themes in the Old Testament: creation, exodus, temple, day of the Lord. But certain acts of the drama are carried over into the New Testament. In many respects, in biblical terms, much of the future reference and anticipation center on the coming of Jesus Christ, which in New Testament terms is an event of the last days. Imagery of the day of the Lord, the land, Israel, even of the promised culmination of history, are all at one time or another associated with the coming of Christ (as one example, see themes present in the Magnificat [Luke 1:47–55]). John 1 even associates Jesus' coming with the original creation. Pointedly John notes, Christ is "the true light, which enlightens everyone," and we "have seen his glory, the glory as of a father's only son, full of grace and truth. . . . And the word became flesh and lived [tabernacled] among us, and we have seen his glory" (John 1:9, 14 NRSV). In his teaching, healing, and feeding the crowds, Jesus fulfilled the Old Testament prophecies regarding God's care for his people: "He will feed his flock like a shepherd" (Isa. 40:11 NRSV). Many Old Testament images coalesce in the course of his teaching. He is the good shepherd (John 10) and the vine (John 15). His favorite self-designation is the "Son of Man," a title that is itself rich in symbolic allusions, including a reference to the Son of Man of Daniel 7, who will appear at the end of history in the clouds of heaven. Could this be the one to whom the prophets look as bringing history to its climax?

In various ways, the Gospel records hint that this is the case. Surrounding Jesus' teaching and miracles are pivotal events accompanied by powerful signs that appear apocalyptic in character. His baptism features a voice from heaven. Later on a mountain he meets with Moses and Elijah and is transfigured before his disciples, his face and garment shining with a brightness beyond the power of any earthly fuller. And then in the great climax of his life, he is lifted up from the earth on a cross, as Moses lifted up the serpent in the wilderness. In this climactic event, he becomes the redeemer of the world and its created splendor. The earth responds with its own dramatic darkness and an earthquake, recalling the earlier interactions of God with his people.

Few events in history have provided the inspiration for such great works of art as has the death of Christ. Like the exodus or the day of the Lord, and indeed related to them, the cross is a central biblical symbol. This human instrument of execution, standing for all the evil that humanity has done to itself, now stands for both the reality of that horror and the redemption and reconciliation that Jesus accomplished through his death. For many people, wearing a cross is little more than a casual choice of jewelry. But such is the case because for these same people sin is not an offense against a holy God, and God's love is little more than a general goodwill toward everyone. For these people the strength of the symbolism of the cross has been lost. Paul spoke of these people in 1 Corinthians 1:18: "The message about the cross is foolishness to those who are perishing"—for such people the cross is a stumbling block rather than a living symbol (Gal. 5:11 NRSV).

The resurrection and glorification of Christ is represented further in an earth-shaking biblical event: Pentecost. At Pentecost God sent his Spirit upon "all flesh," an event signified by pounding wind and tongues of fire. In fulfillment of Old Testament prophecies, Peter says, God is fulfilling his promise of the last days (Joel 2:28). God has come again to the earth in the form of the Spirit to finish the work that Christ began to do in creation. The Spirit of Christ has been sent to empower creation to recover its created splendor to the eternal glory of the Father. Little wonder that three thousand among the astounded crowd responded to Peter's appeal with faith.

A final collection of biblical images is found in the Book of Revelation. This grand climax could well be called a final gathering of all biblical imagery (and poetry) into a single narrative. Put differently, Revelation collects all the biblical narratives and weaves them together into a single series of images that refers to the end of God's project of creation and reconciliation. Revelation in one sense is better sung or danced than read and outlined, for it is only in such dramatic images that the powerful presence of the Triune God, who gathers up all history into the final settlement, is properly experienced. The images constitute the vision that John saw on the Island of Patmos and recorded in this final New Testament book.

These themes of Scripture, each of which could be elaborated at great length, together demonstrate the integrity and coherence of the biblical drama. All of them in one way or another include God's activity and presence, but they also invite the full participation of the creature. In none of them is God a distant, uninvolved deity (as in Deism); at the same time, however, God's involvement in no sense overwhelms the participation of creation. Note how all these themes have aesthetic and visual dimensions. Often these themes result directly in sacred art and imagery (for example, the temple, the Book of Revelation), but equally often they have become a rich stimulus for creative work through the ages. Apparently, there is nothing God does that does not send off sparks of beauty that call attention to his redeeming and loving presence. The world, then, even apart from its interpretation in Scripture, declares the glory of God; it is an embodied witness to this redemption and love. Below we will note the significance of this when considering and appreciating great art that is made by those who deny God.

Images and the Bible

An examination of some of the biblical language for beauty reveals that beauty is connected both to God's presence and activity and to the order that God has given to creation. This coherence and theological grounding is reflected in a particular narrative that emerges from the central themes of Scripture—creation, the exodus, the temple, the day of the Lord, Christ, the cross, Pentecost, and the return of Christ. We are now in a position to ask how visual images function within this biblical context. How are images defined and used in Scripture?

A good place to begin a consideration of biblical imagery is the wisdom writings: Job, Proverbs, Ecclesiastes, Song of Solomon, and certain psalms. In the wisdom literature, we see the concrete embodiment of John Calvin's idea that all of creation is a theater for God's glory. According to this tradition, creation, when it is fulfilling God's intended purposes, has an integrity, a wholeness, that pleases. Moreover, in this order the moral and aesthetic dimensions are both inescapable. A fool may run afoul of this order, but he cannot overthrow it. And while there is a figural splendor to the created order and to revelation, this appears only as a dimension of the whole; it is not something singled out for independent attention.

Consider what is to us a supreme example of beauty: flowers. There is no instance in the Old Testament in which such things are featured and enjoyed in their own right. The Hebrews, in fact, would be puzzled at our focus on such images. A flower cannot be enjoyed on its own for the simple reason that it does not exist on its own. Seen in the context in which it exists, its most remarkable characteristic is that it fades (Isa. 40:8). It may be a bit easier for us to see how a flock of goats running on a hillside, shorn sheep come up from washing, or a strong tower can express the loveliness of hair, teeth, and neck (Song of Sol. 6:5–6; 7:4), but these are not images we would prefer. The difficulty lies in the fact that Hebrew images sought to capture the various roles the objects played in the natural order. As Othmer Keel comments, a person in the ancient Near East had a deep-seated "necessity to show things as they have been experienced by all the senses and internalized through long association."[9] The tower represents purity, pride, inaccessibility, and strength.[10] It brought together all these aspects in a single image. Our modern images feature surface and finish; Old Testament images present structure and character. Modern images are narrow and restrictive; theirs were broad and inclusive. While we are interested primarily in appearance, the Hebrews were concerned with comprehensive content, which for them was a matter both of meaning and beauty. For us beauty is primarily visual; their idea of beauty included sensations of light, color, sound, smell, and even taste.[11]

Israel shared these characteristics with many of her Near Eastern neighbors. But the uniqueness of Old Testament conceptions appears in the comprehensive images that express the unity of creation in judgment and renewal—exodus, Zion, the day of the Lord—which we have reviewed. It is difficult to imagine such a grand harmony and wholeness, for in our postmodern world, we do not often see things as a whole. It is clear from this study that our modern error is at least in part an aesthetic one: We no longer understand the role beauty ought to play in our fragmented lives. Beauty, therefore, expresses our isolation. It does not provide the delight and comfort of integration. It expresses the truth that Hans Urs von Balthasar has pointed out: Where a sense of genuine beauty is lost, the good also loses its force of attraction; and where goodness no longer attracts, beauty becomes a shadow of itself.[12]

While beauty in the Old Testament is often associated with worship, it is possible to overemphasize this connection. In fact, a survey of Old Testament references to beauty reveals that most references have no connection to formal worship (though this does not mean they have no connection to God). As noted above, frequently the beautiful is simply what we would call "the fitting" or "the proper": gray hair on an old man, strength in a youth, virtue in a woman, words well spoken. Here is where the biblical view and the Greek view stand in the greatest possible contrast. In the Old Testament, an object or event is not beautiful because it conforms to a formal ideal but because it reflects in its small way the wholeness of the created order. Something is lovely if it displays the integrity that characterizes creation and in turn reflects God's own righteousness. On occasion, righteousness and beauty are even used interchangeably. Paths of righteousness are simply walkable paths (Ps. 23:3); trees of righteousness are lovely trees (Prov. 11:30). The opposite would be trees that bear no fruit and stony paths, rather than ugly trees and paths.

This humble sense of beauty may be the reason why biblical aesthetics often appears unremarkable. The truth is simply that beauty can hardly be made the object of separate study in the biblical materials without distorting the material. As Eric Werner once observed, beauty occupies a broad borderline between the aesthetic and the moral.[13] The key to much modern aesthetics is the autonomy of form and the purity of aesthetic experience. In the Old Testament, the contrast is not between beauty and ugliness but between beauty in its setting, serving God's purpose, and beauty that is prostituted by leading away from the just order that God intended.

As a result, the experience of beauty was never an isolated, morally neutral experience. Often beauty was related to what we might call "charm."[14] Beauty encourages us to take up a course of action with respect to it. The wise man warns, "Do not desire her beauty in your heart" (Prov. 6:25). And the course of action a person adopts toward this charm surely reflects the allegiance of his or her heart. This is seen clearly in the command against coveting, where aesthetics and ethics show their deep interrelationship. The experiences of the temptation in the Garden and David's episode with Bathsheba display the melancholy progression of beauty as charm. Beauty gives rise to desire, which demands possession. Possession then can destroy the beauty of the object, which lies not in the object alone but in the system of righteous relations it enjoys. The case of Amnon is typical. After he desired David's beautiful daughter and forced her to lie with him, he hated her more deeply than he had loved her previously (2 Sam. 13:15).

This interdependent quality of creation emphasized the lovely mutuality God wished to display. As Claus Westermann observes, echoing St. Francis, the beauty of creation is best understood when creation is viewed as a brother or sister rather than an object.[15] And given this interdependence it is also clear that the proper expression of the fullness of creation virtually demanded a poetic rather than an abstract terminology. As Gerhard von Rad states, "The experiences of reality which confronted [Israel] could be appropriately presented only in artistic form. . . . A whole group of perceptions [of natural phenomena] . . . could apparently be expressed only in hymnic form."[16]

Appropriately, then, in the final settlement, God promises as a part of his judgment to take away the beauty he had given to Israel. She had played the harlot with her beauty (Ezekiel 16; Hosea), and her lovers would themselves strip away her fair jewels (Ezek. 16:39). The false pride in beauty leads to judgment, a judgment in which all beauty is lost: "I take from them their . . . glory" (Ezek. 24:25 NRSV). "All who pass along the way clap their hands at you. . . . 'Is this the city that was called the personification of beauty?'" (Lam. 2:15 NRSV). Beauty and the beautiful, then, are as much the character of an experience or an event as they are of an object. They partake of the larger dimension of the interaction of human and divine life in which all creation plays a part. Beauty can be a sign of blessing, its absence a sign of judgment. Beauty shares in the purposeful movement of a person, a movement in which he or she constantly pulls events and objects into valuing pursuits. It reflects the fact that the Old Testament portrays human life as dynamic, in which each step reflects the delight and the moral seriousness of the whole.

In all references to images, we are struck with this sense of the active participation of God in the world. Since for the Hebrews God was the Creator and sustainer of all life, all things were immediately dependent on his loving care. As a result, they knew no distinction between secular and sacred; it was all given by God's hand. It was natural, therefore, that elements of nature, objects, names, and actions could all be symbolic. Any object had the potential to speak of God's presence in love and judgment, a presence that they always and immediately experienced.

Toward a Biblical Aesthetic

We are now in a position to sum up the biblical attitude toward images and art. People sometimes summarize biblical attitudes by implying that Israel's (and the early church's) experience with God was so spiritual that any dependence on images was avoided as a stumbling block. This reading of Scripture is surely more a reflection of Protestant heritage than it is a result of deep biblical reflection. In the Protestant tradition, hearing the Word of God and following that Word was believed to make all visible assistance unnecessary and even hazardous. Such a view could hardly be farther from the biblical materials we have briefly examined.

The second commandment is often cited in support of the supposed biblical reticence about imagery. "You shall not make for yourself an idol, whether in the form of anything that is in heaven above, or that is on the earth beneath, or that is in the water under the earth. You shall not bow down to them or worship them; for I the LORD your God am a jealous God" (Exod. 20:4–5 NRSV). But this clearly has to do with false worship and not with the attempt to portray religious truth in the form of images. The line is drawn between God and idols, not between God and images. In fact, it could be that God refuses us the right to make an image of himself because he has made such attempts unnecessary (as well as dangerous). God has given, in the created order, adequate reflection of the divine character in the form of the man and woman who were made in God's image.[17] These images are not to be worshiped, of course. On the contrary, they are to call forth praise of the maker (Psalms 8, 19). Moreover, human creators in the Bible are actually commanded by God to make objects that encourage the proper worship of God in the tabernacle and temple, so this activity could not have been proscribed in the second commandment.

But a more telling contradiction to the supposed "spirituality" of biblical worship is the way God's progressive revelation was accompanied throughout by such an impressive variety of visual phenomena and appearances. Frequently, such appearances are introduced by the familiar formula, "And God appeared to . . . ," so that God can say to the people before they cross into Canaan:

> Has any god ever attempted to go and take a nation for himself from the midst of another nation, by trials, by signs and wonders . . . and by terrifying displays of power, as the Lord your God did for you in Egypt before your very eyes? To you it was shown so that you would acknowledge that the Lord is God; there is no other besides him. From heaven he made you hear his voice to discipline you. On earth he showed you his great fire, while you heard his words coming out of the fire.
>
> Deuteronomy 4:34–36 NRSV

Nor does this mixing of the visual and the aural change in the New Testament. As noted, visual signs accompanied Jesus' ministry, and spectacular tongues of fire accompanied Pentecost. Less well known but equally significant is the apostle John's emphasis in 1 John 1:1–3 on that which we have seen and heard and our hands have handled, as a kind of definitive proof for the incarnation itself.

Throughout Scripture the visual experience of God's people was to accompany and elaborate God's Word to them. A direct line extends from Abraham's experience in Genesis 18, through Moses' encounter on Sinai and the cloud and fire in the wilderness, to the splendor of the temple and the visions of Isaiah and Ezekiel, right through to the transfiguration, the crucifixion, Pentecost, and the Book of Revelation. If, as Hans Urs von Balthasar has pointed out, one of God's purposes in the Old Testament is to prepare his people for the actual appearance of God in the incarnation, we can see how vital the visible aspect of God's presence had to be. All the signs of the Old Testament anticipate and prepare for the bright appearance of the Son of God at his birth, baptism, and transfiguration, the darkness of Golgotha, and the shimmering fire and pounding wind of Pentecost. So we can say with von Balthasar that images are not so much prohibited in the Old Testament as integrated into the progressive revelation of God's purposes for the earth, pressed into service as the visible dimension of a transcendent reality.[18]

Finally, an important dimension of biblical symbolism has emerged. Biblical symbols not only unite aesthetic and ethical references and reflect a holistic worldview, but they demand a response on the part of the observer that is more than aesthetic (or even simply ethical). In the last chapter, we noted that Paul Tillich developed a view of symbolism in which symbols opened up a depth dimension of life. All great art is often symbolic in this sense; it opens up windows to the transcendent dimension of life and calls for a response to this dimension. At this point I would argue that Tillich was working out of his biblical heritage and expounding a view of symbolism that is deeply biblical, with this difference: Biblical images demand, when they are placed within their larger biblical context, a response of the whole person not simply to the image but ultimately to God. They call upon one to respond not simply to the images in question but to the Word of God that is embodied in those images. They do not seek only to change one's perception of the world, as all great art does, but to change one's life, something that art alone cannot do. The Gospels, for example, present the narrative about Christ in the form of a challenge and call the hearer to become part of God's story. As John says of the purpose of the Gospels, "These are written so that you may come to believe that Jesus is the Messiah, . . . and that through believing you may have life in his name" (20:31 NRSV).

Herein lies the significance of the visual arts for the Christian. Though there are limits and dangers, we all live our lives in a world that is loaded with symbolic possibilities. Whatever our faith commitments, or lack of them, we live in a world that invariably reflects God's values and even features echoes of his presence. People may miss the significance of these echoes, but as long as they are human they cannot miss the values embedded in creation. And artists by virtue of their special gifts and sensitivities are uniquely able to capture and reflect these values in their work. Even unbelieving artists can lay down deep and profound ethical challenges in their work, as Picasso was famously able to do in *Guernica*—his epic painting about the Spanish Civil War.[19] They are able to encode the joy that lies deep down in the heart of things, as Henri Matisse was able to do in his monumental cutouts. Even in this indirect way, these artists can testify to the grace of God that holds things together in Christ. Though the issues become more difficult here, I can even say that the highest expressions of the art of other religions, when they are good and true, can provide an indirect witness to this common grace.

While Christians can enjoy these gifts and give thanks to God for them, when they do their own work there is more to be said. Based on a Christian's participation in the life of Christ, the mediator of creation and the new creation, his or her relationship to nature is never purely external. The world is the handiwork of the artist's own heavenly Father, and it speaks of his glory. Moreover, Christians are commissioned to share in the program of God whereby the world is being remade into a fit "symbol" of God's goodness. As we have seen, in the Western tradition, the cross has become the central symbol, for it speaks of God's great redemptive love by which he has reconciled the world to himself. But more than this it reminds the believers of their own participation in the death of Christ, who died for "our" sins and in "our" place.

So while all great art is in some sense "redemptive," in that it takes the world and remakes it, Christian artists can understand their work as more directly tied to the work of Christ. As we will note in the next chapter, the work of Christian art can actually be located in God's own trinitarian work of making the world into a fit vessel of his glory. The artist can actually help anticipate the day when the glory of the Lord will cover the earth as the waters cover the sea.

reflecting
theologically
on the visual arts

No biblical reflection is ever done in a vacuum. An earlier chapter revealed that the Reformers refused to consider any visual mediation of the faith, at least in part because of their reaction against medieval practices. Their reading of Scripture, for better or worse, was colored by that historical situation. Our situation is very different. We live in a generation raised on a steady diet of the visual. This, in turn, has raised a wide range of questions that Christians are called to face. Some are troubled by these developments; others are open to the arts in a way that has not been the case for generations. Scripture offers some support, and certain cautions, that relate to our contemporary situation. It reveals, moreover, that the world is laden with symbolic potential that reflects God's purposes and his presence. This symbolism invariably has a visual dimension that can add to its power, and perhaps to its danger.

But now we want to inquire whether there are certain theological categories that are consistent with these biblical materials and that relate them more particularly to our cultural situation. Obviously, this is a large discussion, and it deserves a deeper study than is possible here. But this chapter will call attention to some of the important recent study that has been done, evaluate these discussions, and briefly suggest some further paths.

But first, Why is a discussion such as this important? What does theological reflection contribute to the work of making art? Theological reflection is simply the practice of naming and describing the major commitments that guide thought and action. Artists especially may think they have no need of such "abstract" work, but whether they realize it or not, they inevitably have basic commitments that determine the direction and flavor of their work, even if these are not consciously thought out. This, of course, is true of artists who have no explicit religious commitment, as well as those who do. It is almost certainly the case that every artist is guided by deep and long-term commitments—to the nature of reality, to projects that might improve or more accurately reflect the world as he or she understands it. Many artists seek in their work to call attention to various forms of injustice. Barbara Kruger is a contemporary artist whose work is sometimes considered radical or, some would argue, anarchic. But she is very outspoken about the purpose of her work: "I'm interested in making art that displaces the powers that tell us who we can be and who we can't be."[1] Her work reflects certain deep commitments to freedom from oppression and the misuse of power. Christians, of course, have commitments that relate to God's presence and purposes. In all cases, reflecting on these commitments, even briefly, is essential to giving perspective to the work of Christian art. This chapter reflects on Christian categories in particular and seeks to reveal ways to do art that encompass more of the holism and dynamic of the biblical drama itself.

Incarnation and Glorification

One of the most important claims of the Christian faith is that God entered into space and time in the form of a historical person, Jesus Christ. As the survey of the biblical materials revealed, this implies a great deal not only about the purposes of God but also about God's relationship to the creation. The historical survey noted that a significant part of the church has taken as its starting point and orientation the incarnation of God in Christ. This tradition, represented by the Orthodox and to some extent the Roman Catholic Church, has had an increasing influence over other sections of the church in the last generation. These traditions (or this tradition, since they together made up the first one thousand years of the church) see great significance in the fact that God took on human flesh—took on creation itself—and that with Christ's glorification provided an actual (and in some sense visual) anticipation of God's final work of renewing all creation.

In the Orthodox family of churches, this tradition has placed great emphasis on the holy space, represented by the church building and the images or icons of Christ and the saints that adorn its walls. This space and these images, they believe, together provide a glimpse of the heavenly splendor that is the life of God himself and that Christians will share after death. As we live in this splendor, the Orthodox believe, we can be progressively changed into the image of these saints and their glorious beauty. As the eighteenth-century Russian bishop Theophan the Recluse put this goal, "The principal thing is to stand before God with the intellect in the heart, and to go on standing before him day and night until the end of life."[2] The privileged place to stand before God is the sanctified space of the church in the presence of the images of God's holy ones.

Unlike the Western (Catholic) stream of the tradition, painted icons of Christ, the virgin, and saints came to play a central role in the worship of the Orthodox. Again based on God's own assumption of human flesh, the Orthodox believe that, in a very literal sense, the material world is capable of expressing the infinite. With respect to the saints, God is said to have begun the process of their glorification and continued it after their death. As John of Damascus stated, "The Holy Spirit is never far from their souls, nor from the bodies in their tombs nor from their holy images."[3] The icon, therefore, while not identical with its prototype, became a means of access to it. In fact, Gervase Mathew notes that by the ninth century it had become orthodox to believe that an image was a channel to the person it represented. But as noted earlier, these images were associated in the closest possible way with the sacred sanctuary in which they were displayed (and which in some cases was actually built to house them). In many ways, Mathew notes, the Byzantine Church became itself a single great icon.[4]

In the Catholic tradition, the incarnational focus took a different direction. Rather than seeing the incarnation (and the images that came to reflect that event) by itself as an anticipation of the future glory, Catholics, on the basis of the incarnation, tended to see creation at large as in some way "enchanted."[5] In the last century, Jacques Maritain did important work in drawing out the implications of the incarnation for the contemporary artist.[6] What he called healthy and truly creative intuition exists when an artist seeks and finds herself in objectifying nature in visible matter. Because of God's presence both in nature and in the person, the object and the artist are deeply related. And so in authentic art, the soul of the artist "seeks itself by communicating with things."[7] Since the existence of all things derives ultimately from the divine beauty, the artist can actually produce knowledge in the act of creating, "through which, things and the self are obscurely grasped together."[8] But Maritain worries that the rejection of the transcendent in modern art has produced a void. The modern artist has chosen freedom rather than a delight in beauty and thus runs the risk of denying the true nature of reality, of being antirational rather than super-rational.[9] Rejecting the "connatural" relationship of artist and object, modern art sees subjectivity itself as creative. It does what Maritain calls "self-research," which he finds especially characteristic of surrealism.[10] But art at its best can objectify the creative intuition of the artist, discovering in the work a "value added" that is diffused in the work as a grace.[11] Maritain is helpful in pointing out the deep connection that exists as a result of God's continuing presence in creation based on the incarnation, and the way the best art celebrates what he calls this "connaturality." But if this "connaturality" is a kind of natural or inevitable reality, one wonders how even modern artists are able to deny it. Can this connection be broken, even by those who deny God?

Recently, Patrick Sherry has sought to draw out the implications of this tradition of enchantment for a theology of art based on beauty. Beginning with the incarnation, he notes, "Through the Holy Spirit, God creates beauty that foreshadows the world to come."[12] Because this is true, Sherry believes we need to recover a sense of beauty that has been lost in our contemporary world. Based on God's continuing presence in the Spirit (of Christ), God is somehow present in all beauty. Note that this working of the Spirit is widespread, and our particular discussions of "inspiration," say, of Scripture or of an artist, are fragments broken off the larger whole, which is God's project in creation.[13] Particularly attractive in Sherry's discussion is the special connection of this widespread presence of beauty with the work of the Spirit within the context of the Trinity. This leads him to see the entire world in a new light, as a sign and a sacrament. "If God's being is of surpassing splendor, then it will be refracted and reflected in his creation in a countless variety of ways."[14]

The most significant scholar of this tradition in the past century has been Hans Urs von Balthasar, who Sherry frequently cites. Von Balthasar, whose difficult prose and scholarly isolation kept him out of the mainstream for years, has only recently become widely recognized in discussions of aesthetics. His work is particularly important in trying to put a theological aesthetic (in several volumes) alongside a theology of the true and the good. Like Simone Weil, whom I quoted earlier, von Balthasar wants to begin with beauty because modern people have lost the sense of wholeness that beauty reflects. A recovery of beauty then will lead, he believes, to a recovery of a sense of God. The "good," in fact, has lost its attraction because it has been cut off from beauty. "The testimony of being loses all credibility for the one who no longer is able to discern the beautiful."[15] Though beauty and being have become separated in the modern imagination, their integration was accomplished in Christ, the true Word and image of God, who was not only believed but seen.[16] All that Scripture speaks about (which he calls a "Gestalt") is what Christ started. Is this not what John saw (1 John 1:1ff.)? Is this not the supreme beauty Paul saw on the road to Damascus?

This beauty is tied in the closest sense to "revelation," by which von Balthasar means the reality and impact that emanates from God's work as this is revealed in history and recorded in Scripture. Revelation is, in fact, a kind of calling of creation to order, von Balthasar says, to which we in turn are called to submit.[17] This is based on God's descent into the depths of creation, where he continues to express the mystery of love through experiences of beauty. This beauty is based on the actual and continuing presence of God as the fundamental shape of being. In contemplating this we are ravished by its depths, because there God gives us something to see and hold on to, which enables us to live in an exciting response to his love. Recalling Maritain's connaturality, von Balthasar says, "The aesthetic is then the doctrine of the incarnation of the divine glory and the person called to participate in this glory."[18]

Within this framework, in subsequent volumes he is able to develop a theology of grace in the transcendent experiences of the fear and love of God—all of which echo the great events of the biblical narrative and the glory there displayed (one can see the influence of von Balthasar reflected in the survey of the biblical narrative in chapter 3). God's goal, rooted in the presence of the Trinity, is to bring to realization the concrete glory of God, what von Balthasar calls a "cosmic liturgy," whereby the creature is admitted to the domain of God.

Much here is helpful, even compelling: the continuing connection and investment of God in creation through the continuing work of the Spirit; the founding of aesthetics in the incarnation, with its fusing of God with the creation, even in its fallenness; and especially the recovery of "splendor" and even "glory." These words, in spite of their centrality in the biblical narrative, have become, like virtue or virginity, historical relics. But it could be that the spiritual longing characteristic of this generation may in fact be a longing for glory, a glory that many find in charismatic experiences of worship.[19]

But there are cautions to be raised as well with respect to von Balthasar's cosmic vision. In the comprehensive view that creation represents, even reveals, God's purposes, the dark places are reduced to necessary shadows in the beauty of the whole. There does not seem to be room for a radical expression of sin as calling for a radical reversal and reconciliation that is also the purpose of Christ's appearance. Further, an insistence on the world itself as a sacrament may exaggerate its current status. Better perhaps is Nicholas Wolterstorff's insistence that the world is God's good artifact, in which we are called to stewardly play and work—in its order and its disorder.[20] Wolterstorff would accordingly challenge von Balthasar's insistence that "contemplation" is a central category for aesthetics. This mode of apprehension would certainly be appropriate for a sacramental world, where God may be glimpsed at any moment and in various forms. But if we are embedded in God's artifact, we may be called to more mundane but ultimately more satisfying interaction with creation—in the multitude of ways we are called to be stewards and bring out creation's splendor in many forms. Perhaps, then, in starting with the incarnation rather than with creation, or even with God, the story of the interaction between God and his work may be slightly misread. The center of the story, however important, should not be taken for the whole.

Aesthetics as a Reflection of the Trinitarian Life of God

Another important discussion of theology and art begins with a slightly different description of what is at the center. There is certainly no lack of trinitarian discussion in the sources just reviewed. But in the end, when it comes to thinking about art and beauty, the incarnation controls the conversation in that tradition. Recently, another group of writers has sought to orient the discussion of art and beauty not in terms of Christ's work alone but with Christ in relation to the trinitarian character of God, especially as this is evident in creation and the new creation. Building on the valuable recent work on the Trinity by Jürgen Moltmann, Colin Gunton, and James Torrance, among others, these writers seek to understand the work of creating beauty in terms of the trinitarian relationships as they are demonstrated in God's redemptive program. They use the mutual relations of the Trinity as the lens through which they understand both creation and the artistic process.

These thinkers are not particularly concerned to understand Christ's incarnation as merely involving God's ontological relationship with creation, though they certainly do not want to deny the importance of this relationship. Rather, they want to draw out the implications of the full program of involvement of the persons of the Trinity in creation and in redemption. In this program, the incarnation is only a part of the story, albeit a critical part. In a recent work, Moltmann gave this description of the process:

> The resurrection glory [of Christ] corresponds to the primordial glory of the Son with the Father. Its light also falls retrospectively on the cross, and in his obedience so that the difference between cross and raising is absorbed into the reciprocal glorification of the Son and the Father. The Paraclete, for his part, will then glorify Christ, the Son, by spreading his knowledge and his love. He proceeds from the Father and illumines the Son.[21]

Moltmann sees this process as inclusive of all creation and all the purposes of God. But to fully grasp it, Moltmann insists, one must be at liberty to "leave moral and ontological concepts behind, and to avail ourselves of aesthetic dimensions."[22] Gunton similarly lays out some guiding assumptions with which he works:

> As the particular and free presence of God to the world, Jesus Christ is the basis of the doctrine of omnipresence. But that cannot be adequately conceived without the Holy Spirit, the one by whose mediation the Son became incarnate and is made the means of relating the creation to God the Father.[23]

These thinkers want to understand human creativity in the context of God's Triune relatedness in the world as it was created and as God works in it to re-create and restore its splendor. In many ways they are similar to von Balthasar, but they work on aesthetics from the side of the trinitarian activity of God in creation rather than from the creation side of the process.

Jeremy Begbie allows that it is permissible to start with Christ as the reason for creation and the continuing mediator of it, because this underlines the critical point that our redemption and that of creation is tied up together in the closest possible way. As he says, "We are involved in a common history with the physical world and cannot entertain our own redemption in isolation from it."[24] But this redemption, as well as our handling of creation, must be placed in its full trinitarian perspective to be properly understood. That is, the Holy Spirit proceeds from the Father and the Son to work in creation so as to bring it, through Jesus Christ, to the place where it is able to praise God the Father. Human creativity must be located, then, not in some general call to care for creation but within the call of the Spirit to glorify the Father through Jesus Christ, an activity in which we in our human way are invited to share. Thus, Begbie argues, "Human creativity is supremely about sharing through the Spirit in the creative purposes of the Father as he draws all things to himself through the Son."[25] In this, Christ is the firstfruit, who takes on human flesh and through obedience to the Father offers it back to the Father by the power of the Spirit. The human creator is able by the Spirit to join in this great cosmic renewing, and his work can be touched by the grace of this work.

As a practicing professional musician, Begbie has often applied this perspective to the understanding and practice of music. In his most recent work, in fact, Begbie uses music as a metaphor for the purposes and activities of God in creation. Music, Begbie believes, gives us important conceptual tools, indeed pointers to the very character of God, that take seriously both temporality and materiality. It is precisely the character of God, Begbie believes, that points to the engagement of the Son of God "with spatio-temporal reality, enacted in the history of Jesus Christ and an equally uncompromising stress on the work of the Holy Spirit as the one who directs created reality towards its fulfillment."[26] This enables musicians to see their work not simply as prayer, which is our dialogue with God, but even more as a part of the inner dialogue within the Godhead.[27]

Trevor Hart, another scholar working in this vein, adds an important dimension in a recent article.[28] What is the "value added" he asks of artistic creativity? Secular artists seem to believe that they add to creation by transcending its limitations. Referring to the Greek myth of Prometheus, Hart asks if the artist is a kind of Prometheus, transgressing the limits set on creation by the Creator. This certainly appears to be the case for certain modern artists, he notes. Arnold Schoenberg sought to bend sounds in conformity with the qualities of the human intellect; Wassily Kandinksy sought to express the soul of nature and humanity by abstracting these elements from their usual setting. Hart by contrast insists that we understand the work of artistic creation after the model of the incarnation and the trinitarian work of God visible there.

Hart refers to Paul's description of this work in Galatians 4:6. There Paul says, "Because you are children, God has sent the Spirit of his Son into our hearts, crying, 'Abba! Father!'" The high point of the Word's relatedness to humankind, while Jesus was on earth, lies in the free response of the human Jesus to his Father in the power of the Spirit, which is expressed when he cries, "Abba! Father!" But Hart points out that Paul implies we are all invited to share in this cry, by the Spirit—we are also enabled to call God "Abba." Here is where Hart draws the analogy with the creative act. Responsible creative activity may be considered a kind of subset, or an echo, of the dynamic calling out to the Father that Paul describes. In the artistic creation, the artist, by the Spirit, is enabled to share in the cry of creation, "Abba," wherein the artistic creation reaches for its true end: being transformed into something that can glorify God.

But Hart adds an important dimension of the limits within which this is carried out. "The artistic imagination ventures forth . . . into a world believed to be already rich with actual and potential meaning."[29] This potential becomes both a limitation and a possibility for the artist. But these too must be understood christologically. As Christ takes our flesh with all its flaws and through Spirit-inspired artistry transfigures it, turning it back to us to the glory of the Father, so we are enabled to work within creation as artists. Our art on this model can be truly physical and yet it can be more—it too in a sense can be transformed into an image of grace. This, then, is the value added.

As in the Catholic and Orthodox aesthetics, this stream also wants the work of creation to anticipate in some important way the final renewal of all things, since it is participating in the trinitarian work that will surely bring this about. Art that bears this special imprint of the Spirit will anticipate in space and time, substantially though provisionally, the final transfiguration of the cosmos.[30] This perspective on creativity has much to commend it, and it is imaginatively suggestive, including as it does a larger scope for the activity of God. And from the point of view of the artist, it is extremely important to understand their work with creation in terms of the mediation of Christ and God's continuing presence through the Holy Spirit, as the Father works in the creature. Creation, these thinkers insist, cannot be understood on its own terms. When it is so construed, it is distorted from its true purpose and end, as being shaped by God into a vessel of praise. This sharing in God's trinitarian work surely describes everything a Christian does—the giving of glasses of cold water as much as the painting of church murals. But the artist in a special way works with and in the temporal and material structures of reality. Artists can be immensely helped, indeed inspired, to see their work as working alongside God in shaping the created order in God-honoring ways. But a question we will want to discuss later suggests itself at this point: Do non-Christian artists, when they shape creation in beautiful ways, share in this trinitarian relation in the same way? In different ways? What about those whose work steadfastly denies this presence?

The theological grounding of creative work that focuses on the special relationship between the Father and the Son is illuminating. It puts the work of artists in a larger context. It makes it a part of a larger program in which God works in Christ through the Spirit. But one might ask how we recognize this. And is this important only for the Christian artist? Clearly, in the Catholic tradition the incarnation has lent a sacramental tone to creation, so all artists can be surprised by the discovery of grace—the grace they reflect in their work glorifies God even when they do not intend it. Is this also what these thinkers are allowing? Can Kandinsky and Schoenberg (the two non-Christian artists to whom Hart refers) be taken up into this process of grace? It is not clear. Partly because of the use of Christ's special relationship with God, art itself appears to be taken up into and conditioned by the process of self-giving love. Hart seems to want to allow the created structures to play a bigger role, but he appears to reduce that role by his stress on the trinitarian relations. Still, these thinkers are concerned to underline the independent character of creation, what Begbie calls the "precarious freedom which God has granted to creation."[31] They would claim, however, that this freedom can properly be understood only in terms of God's trinitarian relationships.

Creation and New Creation

The final contribution to the discussion also has a long heritage, stretching back in many ways to the Reformers, John Calvin in particular. Reformed theologians in the twentieth century, taking their cue from the work of Abraham Kuyper and later from Herman Dooyeweerd, sought to understand human activities in terms of God's purposes for creation. They sought to connect especially artistic activities with God's continuing presence in creation in terms of what Kuyper called "common grace," to distinguish it from the special grace of God manifest in the work of Christ. Much discussion among neo-Reformed thinkers has been on the nature of this grace—its connection with the special work of Christ and with the actual presence of God.[32]

But the starting point for these scholars is clearly the order and structure of creation, which was renewed in Christ as an anticipation of the final renewal at the end of history. These scholars want to relate this structure to the work of God, as do the Orthodox and Catholics, but they do not see creation as immediately transparent to God's presence. Indeed, in important ways they would insist that God allows the materiality and temporality of creation's structures to have an integrity and freedom. As God says to creation in Genesis 1, "Let the waters bring forth . . . let the earth bring forth." The work of artists, like all other workers, is responsible to this very physical and this-worldly story of creation that Scripture narrates. And while there is no question of separating the creation from God's continuing activity, it is important, according to these thinkers, to have a clear notion as to what God intended in creation and what has come about in the course of events. H. R. Rookmaaker, perhaps the best-known writer in this group, insists, for example, "This world is God's world. He created it, he maintains it, he is interested in it. . . . Nothing can exist outside of him and all things have meaning only in relation to him."[33] But the context of this statement is the assertion that there is no duality in creation between nature and grace, high and low; God is present and interested in the whole. The real division in creation, in his view, is between the rule of God and that of darkness, which is the result of sin. There is in creation, then, a fundamental disorder that has resulted from the fall and that must be reckoned with. Art inevitably reflects this struggle between the goodness of creation and the disorder and rebellion caused by sin, and so it is invariably theological in this sense.

The story of modern art, as Rookmaaker goes on to describe it, is the story of human artists seeking to make their way in the good world that God has made and in which his grace is still active. Art always portrays the world in a human way and depicts the experience the artist knows. But since roughly the middle of the nineteenth century, artists have lost the larger perspectives of myth and history that gave humanity a larger (and, he believes, truer) sense of itself. They were finally reduced in the twentieth century to making art into a kind of cry of despair. Subsequent writers have challenged many of Rookmaaker's judgments of modern art—Rookmaaker tended to call art that refused to be open to the dimension of God "bad."[34] He sometimes conflated his judgment about the direction of modern art with negative judgments about particular works of art. Certainly, Picasso can sometimes reflect the wholeness of creation and its joy, even if he refused to acknowledge the source of them in God.

But Rookmaaker's overall views may still have validity. Art does surely reflect the spiritual struggle of creation for righteousness and wholeness. Because of common grace, the art of the twentieth century frequently reached a high standard of quality that we can celebrate and enjoy. While we express our admiration, however, we can still insist that this art reflects values that are often contrary to the wholeness and light of biblical truth. But Rookmaaker's thesis goes beyond even this. He insists that we must be engaged with the art we see around us, whatever its orientation. We may not like the art of our time, but we must deal with the questions it raises, even as we are engaged with the culture that produced it. To avoid this is to deny our Christian responsibility. And the most appropriate response from Christians, Rookmaaker argues quite rightly, involves a complete renewal of the church at large.[35]

People are called by God to respond and develop the structures of creation, which Rookmaaker calls "possibilities."[36] These possibilities have been best illumined by the life, death, and resurrection of Christ. Art and culture, then, must ultimately be understood in the light of the Christian story. As a result, there is something that is more important than art: what God is doing in the world. Never try to show the validity of Christianity through art, Rookmaaker says, "rather the validity of art should be shown through Christianity."[37] And Christianity is about the renewal of life (and of creation), so the norms of art are no different from the norms for the whole of the Christian life. "On the foundation of Christ as his Lord and Savior in love and freedom, the Christian acts in accordance with the structure of the world."[38] So that, "Christian art is nothing special. It is sound healthy good art. It is art in line with the God given structures of art."[39] If truth is "the way God does things," as Calvin Seerveld insists, then artists like every-

Pl. 1. *Adoration of the Magi,* Gentile de Fabriano. Alinari/Art Resource, New York. Used by permission.

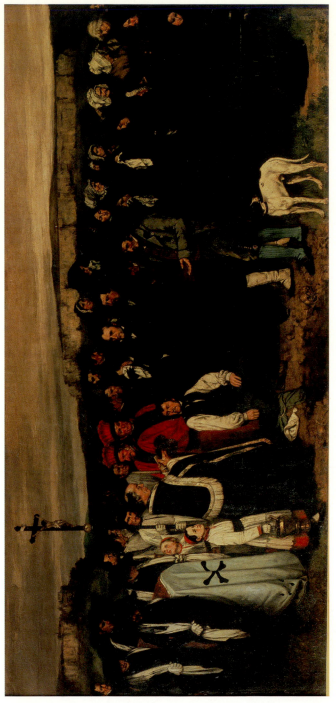

Pl. 2. *Burial at Ornans*, Gustave Courbet. Scala/Art Resource, New York. Used by permission.

Pl. 3. *The Artist's Garden at Vetheuil,* Claude Monet, 1881. Oil on canvas, 39^{5}/$_{8}$ x 32".
© Norton Simon Foundation, Pasadena, California. Used by permission.

Pl. 4. *Futako Tamagawaen,* Makoto Fujimura. Used by permission of the artist.

one else are called to the truth, to do their work in a way that reflects something of the splendor and allusiveness (Seerveld's word) that God intended. But even if the Christian story as portrayed in Scripture defines reality, this does not mean that we cannot learn things from art, for good art is part of the process of uncovering the possibilities God has put in creation. When artists do capture something of the way "God does things," whether they are Christians or not, we are challenged to see the world, and even God's presence there, in ways that we have not seen it before.[40]

A similar point of view is developed in the work of Nicholas Wolterstorff, who wants to start, as noted above, with the world as God's good artifact.[41] He speaks much of the danger of seeing art only in terms of contemplation, which has been institutionalized in the world of high art, where works of art become surrogate high gods.[42] Rather, works of art are objects and instruments of action—they are a part of the way that artistically one acts in the world. Art is a necessary dimension of the way God made the world to work. To deny dance, he says, is to deny an entire dimension of our created being.[43] Revealing a theme that is common in this tradition, he notes that being a good artist is nothing special, for God holds everyone responsible for certain things: being a steward of the earth, loving our neighbor, and praising God. God is working in Christ and by the Holy Spirit to bring about a final shalom, and artists are called to celebrate and anticipate this event (or they can rebel and propose an alternative "shalom"). But the artist, like everyone, is held responsible to God's structured creation.[44] Artists are led along, Wolterstorff notes, in a conversation with their materials.[45] They use these materials to envision and then project a world, inviting us to consider such a world and judge its "fittingness." This projection can be a world that God indwells and loves, or it may be some surrogate gospel of redemption and liberation. While either world may be well or poorly drawn, judgment on the truth or "fittingness" of these worlds is surely a part of the overall evaluation that one makes of the work of art.

Evaluation and Summary

Incarnation, Trinity, and creation—clearly, in many respects these three perspectives complement one another. But each focus is adjusted slightly toward Christ's continuing presence (and the way this has fundamentally changed reality), or the trinitarian activity of God, or the good creation and its structures. In various ways, each tends to see the others as deficient. Begbie has argued that the neo-Calvinist emphasis on the law and rationality of creation obscures the freedom of the creature and seems to constrict even redemption; he rejects the distinction between common and special grace, wanting rather to understand grace relationally and personally. Besides, he would say, it is the trinitarian work of God that allows the creature to be truly itself.[46] Wolterstorff worries that an overemphasis on God's presence in creation tends to make creativity a reflection of God; aesthetics is reduced to expression. This distorts, he believes, the nature of God's good artifact.[47] Von Balthasar, for his part, tries to counteract an overemphasis on questions of truth, which he thinks is possible by focusing on the splendor of God's presence and work in creation.

But each emphasis has something to contribute to the conversation. The emphasis on the incarnation provides an important reminder of the continuing significance of God's entrance into creation. The trinitarian emphasis on the rich interrelationship of God's activities provides an important and biblical lens with which to understand the world. Indeed, I believe it offers an important corrective to the Reformed understanding of creation. The spiritual encounter we moderns yearn for is found only in recognizing and celebrating the ordered relations of creation and our awareness of God in, with, and under these relations. All of this conditions the work of artists as it does any other work we do.[48] Understood in this way, God's purposes, rather than being seen as lawlike, can be understood as potentials within creation, an order in which God is personally invested, indeed, in which he is present.

Still, Reformed thinkers insist that to properly allow for the playful and spontaneous character of art, creation must hold a giant reservoir of possibilities. It must have some kind of integrity that is central and that allows curses as well as songs of praise. And while the stress on the incarnation is helpful in underlining the significance of Christ's continuing mediation of creation, this insight is further enriched by a stronger focus on God's trinitarian activity. Each contributes something important even if its special focus is a potential weakness. For example, if Reformed thinkers are guilty of thinking of redemption in terms of creation, and thus of limiting God's activity and freedom, the trinitarian party runs the risk of reducing creation to the language of "self-giving love" that describes the Godhead. A focus on the incarnation risks the loss of the transactional character of Christ's death with respect to human sin and reconciliation with God. On the other hand, there has been a weakness in the way Reformed aesthetics has integrated the Trinity into Reformed thinking. Amazingly, Rookmaaker makes no reference to the Holy Spirit in his discussion of Christian art. Perhaps more work needs to be done by the Reformed group on what is called the economic Trinity, that is, the way in which God's inner-trinitarian relations are evident in creation and redemption. In this they have much to learn from the scholars who are focusing on the trinitarian relations and creation. Meanwhile, the broader work of the Holy Spirit outside the church can be invoked to connect with some of the insights of Catholics and Orthodox as a way to celebrate the broader purposes of God in creation. While much remains to be done, there is much to celebrate in the deepened conversations among these traditions that have emerged in the last generations.

Toward a Theological Perspective on Art

I can now make some suggestions about a theological perspective on the visual arts that is informed by the brief reviews of biblical and theological precedents. Such suggestions begin with the recognition that artists, even people who enjoy and want to understand the arts, will not necessarily have thought-out positions on the theological themes just reviewed. Indeed, as practitioners their awareness of such positions will often be peripheral and intuitive. Artists, after all, think with their hands and their fingertips, with their eyes and their ears, usually in ways they cannot articulate in words. Their media are shapes and colors. As a result, theological reflection must be oriented to this physical activity. It must inquire into God's possible interest and presence in such practices. The statements that follow, therefore, are meant to move us toward a practical theology of aesthetics and art.

Let us begin with the question, What is the uniqueness of art that distinguishes it from other human activities? As noted above, in an important sense it is "nothing special," and I will return to that point shortly. But it obviously does possess some characteristics that distinguish it from other activities. What are they? The review of Scripture underlined the interconnection of the moral and the aesthetic, and even the merely useful. But what humans do with God's creation, like the creation itself, has ends that cannot be comprehended by examining what is useful or even moral—though the ends will ordinarily relate to these things. Utility, morality, even human development are all important to God, and so they are important vessels to bring to the abundance of creation. But even these vessels sometimes overflow, and work breaks into a song or a dance. Perhaps it calls for a full-color drawing that speaks of the sheer delight or the splendor that God's presence calls forth. This melody, sketch, or dance is a kind of foretaste, an intermediate expression of a final chorus in glorious and dramatic color, that we will perform when we stand before the Lamb, singing our perfected praise. Or perhaps it is a cry of despair over the distance we still feel from that moment of peace. Art can be, in other words, a rest (or even a restlessness) that speaks of Rest.[49] It is a "wondering" that is meant to lead us to the final wonder over the depth and breadth and height of God's goodness, or over the horror of injustice. In its depth it may even reflect some of the urgency of the Book of Hebrews, which warns, "Therefore, while the promise of entering his rest is still open, let us take care that none of you should seem to have failed to reach it" (Heb. 4:1).[50] Art, then, is that human activity that goes beyond the useful to embody in allusive color, shape, or sound the joy or pain of being human.[51] As Wolterstorff stresses, art is a way of acting in the world that engages with its materiality in such a way that it illumines something about the world's depth and reality. It is an activity that involves a way of knowing as well as doing; it shows us something we can learn in no other way.

This value added is possible because there is a depth to things that is ultimately personal. When we cry or exclaim over the beautiful or splendid, we want to share the experience with others. This is because our response is deeply personal, indeed, interpersonal. We are responding in this activity to a call that, Scriptures say, goes out through all the earth (Ps. 19:4). However distant or indistinct, this call is a reflection of God's work in creation, his presence in Christ, and the personal presence of the Holy Spirit, calling and working in the creature to bring it back to the place where it will, in and through Christ, glorify the Father.[52] Having learned from recent trinitarian studies, we see creation through a trinitarian lens. But we insist that, as artists, Christians like everyone else struggle with the materiality of creation. God is the beginning and the end, but this awareness gives us no special access to creation, though it does give us confidence and hope. Our work with creation is part of the freedom that God gives to his children, but it is a freedom that mysteriously turns out to be grounded in his continuing presence.

Artistic practice takes place in a created order that is given its own reality and structure even as it is open to the divine presence. Therefore, a complete understanding of art for the Christian must pay serious attention to the purposes and structures of God's good creation, both as limitation and as potential for the Christian artist. Note that this order does not compete with but complements the awareness of the presence of God described above. God the Father is present throughout creation as the Holy Spirit, witnessing to the redemption that Christ has introduced into the world, seeking to draw all things into that great heavenly pageant of praise. But a Christian view also acknowledges the brokenness of the world and is sensitive to the cries of despair that reflect an order that, precisely because it has been given its own integrity, can resist God's purposes.

Further, the Christian recognizes that being an artist is part of the human challenge of having dominion over the earth, of the call to stewardship—it calls special attention to a particular (aesthetic) way of being human in the world. This follows from what has been said, but it is also consistent with recent findings in both linguistics and art. The picture theory of art, as of language, has clearly been shown to be false. This view, that art may picture some timeless ideal, rested on the classical ideal of Plato that language can reflect and approximate the ideal form. Rather, Ludwig Wittgenstein insisted in the twentieth century that language constructs reality; it does not merely reflect it. Language, the language of art as all others, is meant to do things, not simply to show us something. So Nicholas Cook argues that the meaning of music, and I would add of visual art, lies in what it does rather than in what it represents.[53] Better its meaning lie in what it does *with* what it represents. Just as the meaning of music does not lie in the notes alone but in what the performer does "between the notes," so the meaning of a work of art does not lie with the subject or the colors alone but with what the artist does with these things. And its fuller context includes even the reception of the work by the viewer. To understand art completely, therefore, we have to pay attention to its production and our reception of the work, for art is both a way of knowing and a way of being in the world.[54]

Four statements can summarize this discussion. *Art, as argued above, is nothing special.* It is a part of the response to the call of creation (and of God in creation) that all are called to hear. As is the case with everyone, though in the unique ways described, the artist is to be responsible to what is there, to represent its order (or disorder) in striking or fresh ways in various media, to call the world to attention. But artists always ask themselves, call attention to what? Is there anything worth living and dying for? With striking form, what has been called allusiveness, the artist is able to raise these questions. The special calling of the artist is to call the world to a kind of rest or remind it of its restlessness. This is the value added of art.

But if art is nothing special, it can be a part of something that is. *What is special is God's revelation of himself and the call of creation to praise him in response.* What is really important, of course, is who God is in himself. But our approach to God is only through what he is doing in creation and the new creation—what we can touch, see, and feel (1 John 1). We are embodied creatures and therefore have access to God only in and through creation. In this, God acts as Creator, and in Christ as mediator of the new creation, and through the creative Spirit as one who woos the creature. This working of God in and through creation is what is truly special for us and for everyone else. The call of God goes equally to everyone to respond to this revelation of God: To reflect and embody his purposes with all of his or her life and activity. These purposes of God are comprehensive. They include the whole of life—how we dress, eat, work, play, and, yes, the works of art whose purposes cannot be reduced to any of these activities. All of these can be taken up into the truly exciting program of God that Scripture calls God's reign.

How does art relate to this program of God? *Human art, when it is good, manages some echo of this reality—either to praise or curse.* This does not mean that art cannot be mostly for fun—a quick sketch or shriek of delight in life itself. Even this delights the Creator. Nor does it mean that all art has to aspire to some deep spiritual purpose. But art that is worthy goes with the grain of a God-inspired and Spirit-upheld order, or it stands against this order, or more usually, it stands in some ambiguous relationship to it. Ultimately, the created order holds us accountable, and we either see through it to the loving hand of the Creator, or we make it something of an idol—something that refers only to itself.

The final point is the most comprehensive and perhaps the most controversial. *In some mysterious sense, all art aspires to be worship.* This is not to say that every artist wants to use his or her art to praise God; many emphatically reject the very idea. But they do want their art to witness to something larger than this or that temporary and finite form. Art that is serious always hungers to be a part of something larger; it wants to be a kind of summing up exercise that brings the pieces together and that reflects and comments on the ultimacy of order or disorder—even to celebrate (or perhaps curse) this larger reality. And the world, for its part, is made in such a way that one day every particle of it will contribute its share to the praise of the eternal Triune God. One way or another every artist anticipates that day.

contemporary
challenges
for christians
and the arts

I have argued that Christian views of art grow out of an understanding of a Tri-une God who loves and upholds the world by his Spirit and intervened in Christ to reconcile all things to himself. At the same time, because of its focus on God's good creation and his purpose to create a new heaven and earth, Chritianity is, in an important sense, a worldly and embodied faith. The Christian story focuses on God's love story and his purposes for creation and even for human society—his final purpose being what Paul describes as bringing "all things in heaven and on earth together under one head, even Christ" (Eph. 1:10 NIV). Given these core commitments, how can we understand and respond to some of the challenges from the contemporary arts and popular culture that face Christian artists and thinkers? More importantly, how can we as Christians engage with this world in a creative and constructive way?

In order to answer these questions, we need to review the place the visual arts have reached in the last century or so—some observers might describe this as the corner that contemporary fine art has painted itself into! As noted in an earlier chapter, the division between the high and low arts is breaking down. This blurring of the lines and, one might say, mutual penetration has a great deal to do with the particular course of recent developments in what are called the fine arts. Thomas Crow, who has written tellingly of the relationship between high and low, distinguishes the fine arts as "a highly specialized activity requiring considerable learning and patient application from its practitioners and primary audience," from those arts that have a wider appeal.[1] To oversimplify, one can say that since the mid-nineteenth century, art has shed much of its symbolic or mythological content and has progressively narrowed its focus, thinking only of form, or the elements of design, or even color. We will see how these developments contributed to the rapprochement between the fine and popular arts and at the same time promoted and reenergized popular culture. The latter, in turn, often provided inspiration for the fine arts.

The Nineteenth-Century Background

Since the seventeenth century there had been a strict hierarchy of the visual arts. Growing out of theory that developed during the Renaissance, this order was based on the assumption that "painting fulfills its highest function in a representative imitation of human life, not in its average but in its superior forms."[2] Painting was enlisted in a noble cause: not only to instruct and delight but to inspire an imitation of the highest forms of human life. This view was reflected in the hierarchy that the French Academy canonized in the 1660s. History painting, whether biblical or mythological, was the highest form, followed by portraiture, and finally by what was called genre, or paintings of everyday life. All these forms, however, were meant to embody an order, or decorum, that the audience could understand and emulate.

Beginning early in the nineteenth century, however, this hierarchy and its purposes were both systematically flouted. An important figure in this development was Gustave Courbet (1819–1877), who painted ordinary scenes of everyday life—which were decidedly not edifying—on an epic scale. A socialist and revolutionary, he wanted to convey that the lives of ordinary people counted for just as much as those of kings and priests. Little wonder the public was shocked. Plate 2 shows a burial not of a religious or political leader but of an ordinary person. Nor was the presence of a priest in the picture significant for Courbet (he was violently anticlerical); he simply needed, he said, a touch of red in the picture! This scene and this burial, he insisted, are as worthy of our attention as any other. All visual interest is the same.

In a way, these ideas were part of a larger movement during the nineteenth century, influenced by Romanticism and known as Realism. Artists influenced by Courbet, soon excluded from the regular exhibitions put on by the Academy, began to organize their own Salon des Independents. Between 1874 and 1886, eight critical exhibitions were held in Paris that featured prominently artists who came to be called Impressionists. Rejected by the artistic establishment, these artists felt they were discovering something true and noble about the world. But this nobility was not a product of religion or tradition—both of which were seen as oppresssive—but of discoveries made within oneself. One such artist, Camille Pissaro (1830–1903), wrote to his son Lucien in the 1880s,

"I am enchanted by painting and art in general. It is my life, and makes up for everything else. When one makes a thing with all one's heart and all that is noble in oneself, one always creates something that is recognizable."[3] He urged Lucien to keep drawing what was before him with simplicity. He spoke frequently of the way the authorities mistrusted these artists and held on to old beliefs. These "superstitions," however, were no longer needed. The Impressionists, Pissaro noted, had the true position. They stood for a robust art based on sensation, which was an honest stand.

Honesty with a touch of innocence was surely what appealed to the crowds who attended these exhibits, and especially the Americans who became the first major art market for these artists (and who continue to flock to exhibits of Claude Monet or Impressionism). But there was an irony in this artistic movement that anticipated developments of the twentieth century. On the one hand, the work exhibited a celebration of surface beauty and color, a celebration of the honesty of life and reality. At the same time, this artwork revealed a thinning out of that reality, a gradual elimination of depth and ground or reality—since these images were no longer "symbolic" of any larger dimension of reality. This did not happen immediately, nor all at once. But the struggle between the surface and the depth, and the accompanying struggle over the nature of symbolism, soon became evident in the work of the Post-Impressionists.

Originally, Impressionism triumphed because it celebrated the "visual curtain rather than the conceptual bulk,"[4] as William Seitz put it. The first critics were enraged, teasing these artists with the term "Impressionism," since their work was anything but impressive! What the dour critics who despised these early paintings did not recognize was that openness to the world on its own terms is a bracing experience. And we would be ungrateful if we did not join in this celebration. Claude Monet's (1840–1926) *Garden* (pl. 3) represents a kind of fugue of color and purple shadows and moves us by its brightness and even by the reassuring warmth of its shadows. A warm and comforting presence often comes through in these works. And we are tempted to sing with Gerard Manley Hopkins, a contemporary of these artists:

> Glory be to God for dappled things—
> For skies of couple-colour as a brindled cow.[5]

Perhaps we are enthralled with the people in these paintings who are being themselves so effortlessly. In our labored lives we envy them. Here is the reason Impressionism has such a timeless appeal: People are always drawn by what is super in the natural. When one looks carefully at what is there, it is possible to know that "the world is charged with the grandeur of God,"[6] even if, as is true of these artists, God does not figure in the equation.

Impressionists sought the surface but were not able to provide, from history, mythology, or theology, any substantial foundation for this bright surface.

G. K. Chesterton complained that the world of the Impressionists seemed to have no backbone.[7] One might say that these artists explored the texture of creation and found much to celebrate. But the real question these painters raised is whether, in the long run, one can hold on to the surface without some sense of the depth. Can one hold on to the particular without also acknowledging the One who holds it together and even shines through it? Is this connection dispensable? Can the particular we celebrate survive without its larger context? Robert Pippin sees this as an attack on traditional notions of coherence: "The modern positing of the particular loses that particular, for it deprives it of concrete subsistence and meaning."[8] Though it took more than a century, clearly Impressionism started modern visual art down the path where it struggled with the tension between surface appeal and deeper meaning, or between autonomous form and a broader content (what we used to call "reference"). But from its beginnings until its final burst of energy in the 1950s and 1960s, modern art continued to draw crowds; indeed, the giants of that early period, Monet and Vincent van Gogh (1853–1890), have become heroes of popular culture. It was all great fun, as long as you didn't look too closely! An interesting testimony to this comes from the youth subculture of the 1990s featured in the movie *Clueless*. "Monet" is a term that describes something that looks good from a distance but is a mess up close!

This tension soon became evident among the Impressionists themselves, as one can see when wandering through an exhibit of their work. Some, such as Georges Seurat (1859–1891) and Paul Signac (1863–1935), tried to make Monet's small brush strokes into an artistic program. This soon became a kind of *reductio ad absurdum* of Impressionism's search for freshness of style. People (and artists) began to lose interest. On the other hand, Post-Impressionists, such as Paul Gauguin (1848–1903) and Odilon Redon (1840–1916) and later Paul Cézanne (1839–1906), realized that the bright colors had to carry more than their surface weight. They had to convey a deeper sense of things; they had to retain some symbolic connection. But the artists had no clear view of what this should look like. Gauguin traveled to Tahiti in search of purity and primitive life (and myth?) that he had lost; Redon sought meaning in fantastic images inspired by Edgar Allen Poe; Cézanne, who was to have the biggest impact on twentieth-century art, sought with greater success the geometric and structural depths of the surface beauty.

These countercultural artists created what became known as the avant garde of the art world. Though initially despised by the cultural establishment—most were specifically excluded from the major salons—they often connected with the common people, who crowded into their shows. The Impressionists and the Post-Impressionists illustrate the fact that innovation in culture is often found at the margins and that it frequently grows out of what can best be called popular culture. As with any cultural innovation, the impact of this movement was ambiguous. From one point of view, this was a very creative period in the development

Fig. 19. *Nude Descending a Staircase, No. 2,* Marcel Duchamp. Oil on canvas, 1912. Philadelphia Museum of Art: The Louise and Walter Arensberg Collection. © 2001 Artists Rights Society (ARS), New York/ADAGP, Paris/Estate of Marcel Duchamp. Used by permission.

of modern culture. These artists expanded the scope of subjects and media that art could explore. They introduced novel techniques and became open, in ways art never had been before, to influences from outside the West. In many ways, this opennness contributed to the creative explosion of media and popular culture in the twentieth century. But from another point of view, the Impressionists, while they opened certain doors, closed others and started art down a path that ended in a cul de sac. This would not be evident immediately because, while the artists had given up on any intellectual or religious tradition, they did not initially give up on narrative, perspective, beauty, or even craftsmanship—all notions critical to the traditional study of art and its history. But as we will see, each of these in turn became the target of this "liberating" force for change that is called the avant garde.

The Twentieth Century and the Search for Visual Truth

Americans were immediately attracted to the cheery brightness of Impressionism, and under its influence, similar styles developed in American regional art, especially that of California. But with a few exceptions, American artists played no role, initially, in the struggles described. Modern art did not arrive in America until 1913, when over three hundred works of contemporary artists were displayed in a famous exhibit called the Armory Show. Thousands of people visited this exhibit of modern works, about a third of them European, in New York and subsequently in Chicago and Boston. Among these was a work entitled *Nude Descending a Staircase* (fig. 19) by Marcel Duchamp (1887–1968), who was to have a major influence on the art of the twentieth century. Influenced by contemporary scientific studies of motion, Duchamp attempted to show the figure at several stages of its descent, rather than frozen in time. The incredulity with which works such as this were met was famously illustrated by a remark attributed to Teddy Roosevelt: The work resembles an explosion in a shingle factory. Nevertheless, the exhibition exercised an enormous influence on American art, especially in challenging traditional notions of representation.

Duchamp among others meant to challenge not only traditional subject matter but accepted notions of art altogether. He asked questions crucial to the direction the art world would take in the twentieth century. Why are only certain subjects deemed worthy of representation? Why should a figure be shown only in one place or position? Is there no way that art can capture the visual structure of movement (the moving picture was being developed during this time, and Duchamp himself was influenced by serious studies of time and motion)? In 1917, Duchamp displayed a urinal entitled *Fountain* in an exhibition and raised the stakes in the discussion. Initially ascribed to R. Mutt, the work was ignored at first. But when the real artist was discovered, someone celebrated as a famous avant garde artist, the work could not be ignored. In pressing the question What is art? he was also asking about its relation to life, as well as questioning the connection between art and beauty (or significance). In one sense, Duchamp in his own work was making the radical shift that characterizes the twentieth century: the shift from object to concept, from an emphasis on perception to a focus on consciousness. Michael Rush describes his importance in this way: "Duchamp's radical shift of emphasis from object to concept allowed for multiple methods to be introduced to a redefined artistic enterprise. His importance . . . rests not only in what he did but in what he allowed or initiated in art."[9]

A contemporary of Duchamp's, René Magritte (1898–1967), raised the stakes even further by pushing the question of the relationship between image and reality, as is evident in his famous work *The Treachery of Images (This Is Not a Pipe)* (fig. 20). In the context of our discussion, it might be helpful to describe Magritte as a twentieth-century iconoclast. Similar to the earlier iconoclasts, he wanted to challenge the accepted notions, what he would call "superstitions," connected with images. Like the eighth-century iconoclasts, Magritte joined the struggle at the level of the fundamental question, What is the relationship between image and reality? And like the earlier iconoclasts, he called into question that supposed connection. Reality, he seemed to say, cannot be captured.

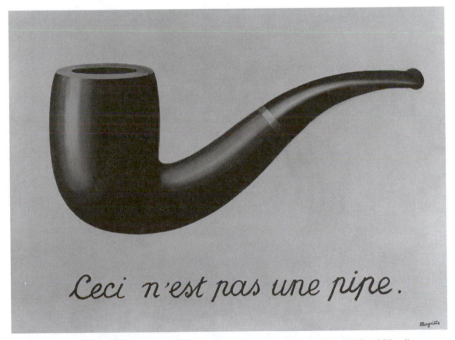

Fig. 20. *The Treachery of Images (This Is Not a Pipe)*, René Magritte, 1928–1929, oil on canvas, Los Angeles County Museum of Art, purchased with funds provided by the Mr. and Mrs. William Preston Harrison Collection. © 2001 C. Herscovici, Brussels/Artists Rights Society (ARS), New York. Used by permission.

And if you think it can, you must remember that the image is not what is real. But unlike previous iconoclasts who wanted jealously to guard God's aseity from any vulgar representation, Magritte had no transcendent faith to fall back on. He did not conduct his deconstruction in the name of any positive vision of the future. Nevertheless, the title of his work pushes the viewer to reflect on reality at a deeper level than the image. If this is not a pipe, what is it? And what is its possible meaning? The art that he made and influenced was shaped under the impress of this fundamental question—a question that was to occupy artists of the next generation. Needless to say, not only did a Christian worldview play no role in the development of this art, but Christian observers were mostly puzzled by it. But could they ultimately ignore the questions that were being raised?

America and the Future: Art after World War II

Whether Duchamp and Magritte were opening the door to new ways to think about and do art, or whether they were destroying the notion of art as it had been known, became at once a matter of intense discussion. But after World War II it became clear that if they were indeed opening the way to new styles of art, the United States would be the place where the changes would happen. In the United States, novelty could be celebrated—in a way untrammeled by the superstitions of the past. During the war, many of the best artists fled from the devastation of Europe to the relative peace and, more importantly, the free-

Fig. 21. *Convergence*, Jackson Pollock, 1952, oil on canvas, overall 93$^1/_2$ x 155", Albright-Knox Art Gallery, Buffalo, New York, gift of Seymour H. Knox, Jr., 1956. © 2001 Pollock-Krasner Foundation/Artists Rights Society (ARS), New York. Used by permission.

dom that America offered. There they influenced a generation of American artists, and New York became the focal point for the developing modern art.

Two movements in particular illustrate directions that the openness of Duchamp took. In a sense, these directions represent the continuation of the tension found inherent in the Impressionist movement—specifically the struggle between inner and outer meaning. But they also explore a different tension, that between high and low in art. In a sense, Impressionism had exploited traditional painterly means in the service of making the picture an improvement on what life could offer. Later movements such as Cubism and Duchamp's Dadaism gave up on the traditional means but still exploited the "idea" of high art, in the service of the contingent and ephemeral—pieces of newpaper or images from everyday life.[10] The tension between these "popular" means and the institution of high art would drive the developments we explore now.

The first movement, Abstract Expressionism, represents an inward quest and an exploration of new forms of consciousness. The most famous artist of this movement was the American Jackson Pollock (1912–1956), who was strongly influenced by European developments, especially Surrealism, with which Magritte was identified. Surrealist thinkers and artists sought to be liberated from the tradition that, like the realists before them, they perceived as oppressive and dead. Religion was, in their minds, one of the things that held people in bondage and needed to be overthrown. As Maxine Alexandre put it in 1930, "The religious spirit is that body of sentiments and ideas which tend to maintain man a prisoner of himself and of other men."[11] The goal was to escape from these restrictions by using dreams, subconscious images, and free-flowing writing as ways into some other (super)reality, which they believed was the realm that would resolve the contradictions of existence. Surrealism, like Abstract Expressionism after it, focused more on the process of externalizing consciousness than on the resultant work of art. "It is axiomatic in Surrealism that the act of creation is in itself only of secondary importance," explains J. H. Mathews. "What really counts is the state of mind the creative act reflects and permits to become exteriorized."[12]

In Pollock's work, this led to "action painting." The work of art as object is not what is important; what matters is the process—or action—of painting, which uncovers what is within the artist. Pollock would place a painting on the floor and drip paint on it, controlling the process while making use of the chance effects that were produced, as in his painting *Convergence* (fig. 21). Such actions were meant to underline the faith these artists had that resolution of the contradictions of life would come from within the human consciousness and not from somewhere outside it. The very idea of "convergence" indicates their implicit goal. Through accidental and unconscious processes, they hoped for a convergence of means and consciousness that would resolve the contradictions of life. Ironically, an eager public came to see these works in ways that

Fig. 22. *Brillo Box,* Andy Warhol. The Andy Warhol Foundation for the Visual Arts/ARS, New York/Art Resource, New York. Used by permission.

recall Impressionism. It is questionable whether they found in them a spiritual process with which they resonated, but viewers liked their decorative character and celebrated their untidy and lavish energy. Again the embrace of popular culture was not long in coming: One of Pollock's early works was used as a background for a *Vogue* magazine fashion shoot![13]

But other artists were all too eager to exploit, and perhaps subvert, this surface appeal. These artists represent the second movement called Pop Art. During the 1950s and early 1960s, a group of artists focused on the detritus of modern life, especially the omnipresent advertising images that proliferated in the postwar boom. The most famous and enduring of these artists was Andy Warhol (1928–1987), who executed large prints and stenciled pictures of Campbell soup cans or constructed large models of Brillo boxes (fig. 22). If Abstract Expressionism was an intensely personal mode of expression, the Pop artists sought refuge in the most impersonal of styles. Roy Lichtenstein reproduced maudlin comic strips; Claes Oldenburg created giant "sculptures" of pants and hamburgers. Viewers were forced to consider the objects of their everyday life as art, indeed, to rethink the concept of high art altogether in the light of proliferating and inescapable advertising (and later television) images. Such works of art were placed in a gallery in such a way that one had to walk around them and consider these everyday objects made to an almost human scale. Once again, as with Impressionism, the energy of innovation was coming from the margins of what had been considered high art, in this case from the commercial culture around it. The engagement of true artists with this world was truly revolutionary and, indeed, controversial. But it was the first stage of what would become a very important development: the growing interaction between commercial culture and the traditional arts.

For our purposes, notice carefully what these movements represent. First, there was a progressive elimination of any pretensions associated with the image. These artists were asking, If the image is not "symbolic," that is, if it is not connected with some other or transcendent reality, what importance does it have? Either the idea of the subject of art must be eliminated, as in the case of Abstract Expressionism, or it must be radically reconceived, as in Pop Art. Notice also that the traditional association of art with craft and skill was being called into question. Now creativity was associated with the entire process and, inevitably, with the personality of the artist, rather than with the resulting work. Similarly, the ancient idea of connoisseurship was being questioned. Enjoyment of art no longer required special preparation or background; indeed, the goal became art that was accessible to everyone. But could such art still be called fine art?

Needless to say, critics greeted these movements with mixed feelings. If everyone was invited to the art party, what would become of the critic's role of introducing and evaluating works of art? This puzzlement is illustrated by the ambivalent relationship between these artists and the dominant mode of art criticism of the twentieth century, what was called formalism. Formalist critics argued that the values of art are concentrated in the work itself, without any reference to the broader world. As one of the early theorists of formalism Clive Bell put it, "The representative element in a work of art may or may not be harmful; always it is irrelevant. For, to appreciate a work of art we need bring with us nothing from life, no knowledge of its idea and affairs, no familiarity with its emotions."[14] The work must be appreciated for its own formal qualities, whether the subject is recognizable or not. This is a clear example of Nicholas Wolterstorff's characterization of the reduction of modern art's role to "contemplation."

In mid-century, Clement Greenberg became the arbiter of taste for the postwar generation, insisting that the meaning of a work of art must be found within the piece itself and not somewhere else. The (usually) formal qualities of the work itself provide the only possible justification for its being. A modernist work, he decreed, must not depend on any outside experience. "This means, among other things, renouncing illusion and explicitness. The arts are to achieve concreteness, purity, by acting solely in terms of their separate and irreducible selves."[15] The goal was an experience that was *sui generis,* having its goal in itself. Clearly, these modern masters and their many followers, whatever their intentions, were creating experiences that for many people became a substitute for religion. In fact, in the twentieth century, experience of art became for many people a kind of secular faith. This may not have been envisioned by the artists themselves; it was discovered after Andy Warhol's death that he regularly attended Mass at the local Catholic church!

But there is a serious irony here that foreshadows the direction that art was taking. Though Greenberg virtually canonized Pollock,[16] both Pollock and Warhol were breaking with the idea that the only meaning of a work lies in its formal qualities. Their aesthetic actually denied primacy to the visual or perceptual elements of art. Some New York and California artists became so upset with such formalist restrictions that they began to repudiate a focus on the canvas altogether. One of these, Allan Kaprow (1923–), sought to return art to life by developing his conception of "happenings." He would gather a group of people in a gallery, as he did in Portland in the early 1970s, where I was present. He divided the group into pairs of people and gave each couple two mirrors, one very small in size and another large, such as would hang on the inside of a closet door. We were told to go into the street and walk in opposite directions until we couldn't see each other. We were then to return and report our experiences. As he wrote in *Art News* in 1958, "Pollock's near destruction of [painting] may well be a return to the point where art was more actively involved in ritual, magic, and life."[17] From the formalist point of view, such talk was pure heresy, but formalist critics, indeed critics of any kind, were no longer calling the shots.

Notice what Kaprow was implying. Since the search for pure image or experience, represented by Pollock, led to a dead end, we must repudiate the entire notion of separating art from the hopes and dreams of life. Rather, we must find a way to reconnect these things. In many ways, this became the driving force behind the art of the 1980s and 1990s. Notice too the way this drive connects contemporary art with the motives of the Impressionists. Art should not comprise a separate compartment isolated from the hustle and bustle of life; it should somehow invade that world and capture its life and search out its meaning.

Whatever the responses artists have given to this quest, whatever the means they have employed, Christians should have no doubt about the validity of the questions being asked. Our view of God's presence in culture is such that we believe, sooner or later, the most gifted and sensitive members of the arts establishment will ask the right questions. And we must be ready to hear them.

The Collapse of the Avant Garde

Abstract Expressionism and Pop Art represent a defining characteristic of late-twentieth-century visual art: the elimination of the boundaries between high and low culture (and, to a lesser extent, among the arts). These developments did much to create the situation we face in the arts at the beginning of a new century, especially with regard to what is called the avant garde. In traditional discourse about art since the Renaissance, high art was distinguished, by the hierarchy of its subject matter and the sophistication of its means, from the popular arts of the people. The fine arts ordinarily involved training and specialization. Since the Industrial Revolution in particular, the guardians of culture have jealously guarded their preserve against the incursion of mechanically produced and thus degraded images and objects. Only handmade objects created by "artists," they argue, deserve to be treated with respect as art. Only the sacrificing (and usually starving) creator should be given the epithet of artist—these few were endowed with "inspiration" to which people increasingly looked for guidance. These became the pioneers of the future and in the nineteenth century became known as the avant garde.

Before the Renaissance, artists were never called "creative." Indeed, *creation* was a term reserved for the domain of God—any human attribution of creativity was considered blasphemous. This was consistent, incidentally, with the biblical usage of the words for "create" and "creator." Such words were used in reference to God alone; they were never used in regard to human artistic activity. In this sense, human artwork was seen as a kind of stewardship of the creative order, or the religious tradition, not absolute creativity. Workers on medieval cathedrals would have been uninterested in being called "creative." They were at home in a rich and growing tradition. They had learned this tradition through long years of apprenticeship and zealously followed the lessons they had learned.

But all of this began to change during the Renaissance and was completed during the Romantic movement of the nineteenth century. In the romantic view, artists were "inspired" by a divine (or quasi-divine) influence and thus enabled to see farther and deeper than ordinary mortals. This idea of creativity lay behind the notion of the avant garde during the time of the Impressionists. These pioneers were artists specially endowed with gifts to see into the future. We see the outlines of this view in Camille Pissaro's statement that one must put oneself into the painting and find there a counterpart of oneself. This view in one form or another is one to which most artists in the last hundred years would have subscribed.[18]

But notice what this implies. What is important is not the perceived qualities, even the visible image at all, but the way in which the image embodies the creativity of the artist. Contrary to formalist theory, the value of a work of art depends not on its objective qualities but on its success in capturing the truth of the artist. The perceptual characteristics are simply the by-products, the epiphenomena one might say, of the creative act. For artists who hold this view, the work of art inevitably becomes a moral, even a spiritual, entity.[19] It conveys the spiritual vision of the artist. So while they are often not religious in any formal sense, many modern artists seek to embody a spiritual vision in their work.

This view was classically explained by Wassily Kandinsky (1866–1944) in 1913. In one of the most famous writings about modern art, Kandinsky described the situation as he saw it in his booklet *Concerning the Spiritual in Art*.[20] There he described the creative members of a culture in terms of a triangle in which a lone creative genius—he used the example of Beethoven—stands at the top, peering into the depths of spiritual truth, with a few followers below him. Below them are artists (or better artisans) of various kinds, and the crowd at the bottom is the audience, struggling to understand what the master is doing. Kandinsky believed that over time this triangle would move forward so that a hundred years after Beethoven many in the audience would see what he saw, while others would stand at an even more advanced apex, peering into the future and leading the way. Influenced by his study of theosophy, Kandinsky believed that if artists would give free rein to their finer feelings, the internal (that is, the spiritual) truth of art would be revealed. All the arts together, then, were contributing to this spiritual pyramid, "which will some day reach heaven."[21]

Kandinsky represented a growing number of modern artists who, early in the twentieth century, were influenced by spiritual concerns, in his case the theosophical movement. Others among his colleagues turned to Swedenbourgian religion, even to Eastern Orthodox or Catholic traditions for nourishment. They illustrate the beginning of a development that by the end of the century was inescapable: a deep spiritual sensitivity among many practicing artists. But Kandinsky's spiritual sensitivities were not only expressions of a personal quest but also support for the cultural role of the artist as a lonely prophet and, of course, the uniqueness of "high art."

By the time we get to postwar art in the United States, the situation has changed dramatically. Pollock and Warhol, of course, were still lionized by the artistic establishment and in many ways continued to play the role of the inspired artist in the romantic sense. But the walls were being breached; Kandinsky's triangle was collapsing. The purveyors of popular culture reached out and embraced Pollock's art—the time between the "daring" moves of the avant garde and acceptance by an eager public having shrunk to zero. Crowds attended the exhibitions of Pollock and later Warhol in New York, and these artists became the darlings of the press. In Warhol, the "artist" reached out to embrace the images of popular culture and enshrine them in the sacred spaces of the Museum of Modern Art. The public for its part thronged into the sanctuary.

By the early 1970s, it had become clear that the idea of the avant garde no longer made sense. Observers were less clear about whether this development was a good thing or a bad thing. Robert Hughes lamented that its demise indicated that we were at the end of our rope culturally speaking.[22] He argued in 1972 that artists no longer sought to "keep up," for the game no longer seemed worth playing. As for the conceptual art that had become popular, "there is," he believed, "no aesthetic criteria for dealing with such works."[23] Sculptor Robert Smithson is typical of many who believed that "the hard thing to face is not that the emperor has no clothes; it is that beneath the raiment, there is no emperor."[24] More sophisticated analyses, such as one by James Ackerman, pointed out that the real problem was that there was no longer a fixed tradition over against which the avant garde could define itself. Gustave Courbet was the first artist who insisted that to do nothing is to go backward.[25] One must move forward by responding to the traditional. But by 1970 there was no "traditional" to argue with. American artists now readily embraced the notion that all important things come out of the future and not from the past and so exercised a revolutionary shift in fashion "from a posture of rejection to one of acceptance."[26] Indeterminate change had become a positive value in itself. The search for the new had become an end

Fig. 23. *Untitled,* Donald Judd, 1977. Los Angeles County Museum of Art, purchased with funds provided by the Modern and Contemporary Art Council and Robert H. Halff. Photograph © 1995 Museum Associates/LACMA. © Donald Judd Foundation/Licensed by VAGA, New York, New York. Used by permission.

in itself. As a result, the public, being open to anything, provided no inertia against which artists could react.

These developing attitudes prepared the way for the movement in the 1980s called postmodernism.[27] Here the voracious appetite of the public provided stimulus for artists to explore an enormous variety of styles and even return to a focus on the "figure" and historical subjects. In tacit aknowledgment that modernism had reached a kind of dead end, artists began exploring a multiplicity not only of styles but of materials and interactions—installations, performance pieces, body art, and video art proliferated. A significant movement that actually preceded the 1980s but continued to exert its influence in the 1990s was Minimalism. In some ways, following Warhol, these artists sought to reduce their work to a minimal statement, as though seeking to go back before or beneath the glitter that had attached itself to art to find some pristine reality. As minimalist sculptor Carl Andre stated, our culture contains too many objects and now "requires significant blankness, some . . . tabula rasa . . . some space that suggests that there is significant exhaustion."[28] Donald Judd's (1928–) untitled piece (fig. 23) from the late 1970s is typical: large squares of concrete placed in a line, mute testimony to our heavy industrialized world and our impotence before it. But there is more. The object's openness invites the viewer to walk around, through, and even, as children, to play in the pieces (the ruins?) of industrial culture. Notice the way the viewer is invited to collaborate with the artist, to help complete the work.

Pop Art, Abstract Expressionism, Minimalism—these were perhaps the last coherent developments that deserve the designation "movement," though even that is a stretch. Nevertheless, they became part of the fundamental reservoir that artists of the present generation draw from. An important style that emerged from these movements and continues to fertilize the arts is "conceptualism." As noted, a primary characteristic of twentieth-century art was the replacement of the object with the conceptual aspect of art, of craft with idea. Growing out of the challenges of Minimalism and performance art, conceptual artists created earthworks or environments, or even "situations," which they documented to drive home a political or aesthetic point. Documentation, pictures, diagrams, video/audio recordings became "art" because they challenged perception and altered ordinary ways of thinking and living. Here the objects of the everyday world were not simply presented unmediated to the viewer, as in Pop Art, but were placed into a larger complex of values and relationships that often parodied or subverted previous works of art.

For example, Sherrie Levine in the late 1970s and 1980s created a reputation that was based entirely on copying modern masters. Taking (or retaking!) pictures identical to those Walker Evans had made famous, she displayed them as her own, entitling them *After Walker Evans*. This called into question the idea of originality and helped assert what she called "the uneasy death of modernism."[29] This "conceptual" dimension, which challenges perception and understanding, may characterize the best visual art made in the last generation. Indeed, one might say that all art has become "conceptual" as it stretches its reach into many areas of life (and into other art forms as we will see).

Fig. 24. *Sin (Without)*, Ed Ruscha, 1991, oil and acrylic on canvas, Los Angeles County Museum of Art, purchased with funds provided by the Modern and Contemporary Art Council and the National Endowment for the Arts. Photograph © 2000 Museum Associates/LACMA. © Ed Ruscha Studios. Used by permission.

Julian Schnabel (1951–), for example, was lionized in the 1980s almost like Pollock, who along with Picasso was his inspiration. Broken pottery, abstract splashes of paint (one entitled *Portrait of God*), bits of velvet—claiming no hierarchy of materials, Schnabel used whatever was at hand. The environmental artist Christo (1935–) is perhaps more typical of the postmodern desire to take art back to the people—at least when the people can get to his work. He has draped materials over buildings, bridges, even islands. In the early 1990s, he placed hundreds of large umbrellas near a freeway in Southern California. People were invited to wander among these mushroom-looking objects, play around them, even picnic under them.

Toward the turn of the twenty-first century, though, almost anything could be seen in galleries. Video and installation art seemed to be in the ascendency—usually with a clear conceptual component. The Carnegie International, for example, in November 1999 featured large installations, such as Martin Kippenberger's *The Happy Ending of Franz Kafka's "Amerika,"* a reconstruction of Kafka's employment office with mismatched furniture on an AstroTurf soccer field, and several short films (e.g., by Ann-Sofi Siden). But interestingly, some of the show's newcomers were painters (such as Americans Alex Katz, Laura Owens, and Ed Ruscha). A piece by Ruscha (1937–) serves as an example of a painting making connections outside the work of art (fig. 24). Playing with religious imagery (and words), his deadpan work subverts the message. But in an ironic way, his heavily conceptual image provides a kind of backhanded testimony to the continuing energy that religious imagery possesses in contemporary culture.

Indeed, an openness to religion (even if treated negatively) and spirituality in general is a striking characteristic of the art of this period. Diane Apostolos-Cappadona captured some of this eclectic excitement when she described postmodernism as "the visualization of the new figuralism within the context of a religious sensibility and with the allusion to earlier works of art."[30] In the light of the history of art over the last two hundred years, this openness to spirituality is perhaps the most important recent development. In an important work, critic Suzi Gablik asked, *Has Modernism Failed?* Her answer was clearly yes, for modernism in her view had become over-institutionalized. Worse, it had lost touch with any sense of the sacred or the universal. "Once art no longer lays claim to the dignity of the absolute, it loses its charismatic 'meaning-giving' function."[31] Subsequently, she worried that postmodernism, for all its openness, was empty at the center; it had no integrative vision. For her part, she wanted to reconnect art with its visionary function of healing and integration.[32] Art, as she put it in a later work, needed to be reenchanted.[33] Recent developments suggest that many artists are beginning to agree.

The above discussion underlines the fact that this is a time of uncertainty in the visual arts. Answers to the questions of media, subject matter, target audience, and, most importantly, artistic meaning are up for grabs. What Christians might make of this period in art is the subject of the next chapter.

a new opportunity
for christian
involvement
in the arts

What are Christians to make of the confusion that currently exists in the art world (or worlds!). We have seen a proliferation of forms and styles in the last few decades—conceptual art, environmental art, body art, performance pieces, installation and video art. Moreover, this cornucopia of styles often embraces images and forms of popular and commercial culture. This liberation from a traditional notion of art worries some observers. Arthur Danto, for example, has pointed out that the end of art was in view "when art, as it were, recognized that there was no special way a work of art had to be."[1] One result is that museums have recently begun to put art into its larger cultural and historical setting, placing pieces alongside items from contemporary popular culture, further eroding, in many people's mind, the line between high and low art. In late 2000, for example, the Los Angeles County Museum of Art opened one of its most extensive exhibitions entitled "Made in California: Art, Image and Identity, 1900–2000." While a substantial number of people attended the exhibit and enjoyed the panoply of objects—surfboards, record jackets, and tennis shoes, mixed in with contemporary artworks—critics fumed that art was being dumbed down. Christopher Knight lamented that the exhibit "radically simplifies works of art, inventing pop literary contexts that dumb them down into false easy-to-read sound bites. By contrast, powerful exhibitions maximize art's complexity."[2] Even the *New York Times* weighed in with its jeremiad. Critic Robert Smith

121

attacked the Los Angeles show and similar ones in New York. Museum curators are becoming merchandisers, he noted. To these curators, "all objects are created equal, all present equally significant amounts of history, none should be 'privileged' above the others." But this demeans art, he insisted. "Why not simply let art be art? It should be enough to honor its specialness, its mysteries, and allow it to work its effect."[3] But clearly, rather than denying the "specialness" of art, these curators were seeking to connect art with its context; indeed, they were suggesting we broaden the categories by which we think about art.

On the other hand, if art is not characterized by a certain "specialness," neither is it limited in what it *could* be. Perhaps rather than demeaning the arts, this enlarged perspective expands their scope and potential influence. As an illustration, we might ask what "sculpture" amounts to in such a liberated environment. It need not be made of traditional materials such as wood or stone. Clearly, it need not refer only to itself, since formalist restrictions have been overthrown. It may connect with other arts, especially, in performance pieces, with dramatic art. It may harken back to a previous era and recall a previous event. In short, it is free to do and be many things.

The Christian who is concerned about making a convincing, rational presentation of the gospel will complain that "standards" are gone and there is no way to communicate universal truth. But the other side of this is that both artists and viewers are now open to new experiences in a way they have not been previously. They are prepared to see new combinations of things that may spark insight or even a fresh realization of God's claim on their lives. Sculptor Lynn Aldrich believes such an environment provides an unusual opportunity for the Christian artist. For a sculptor in particular, she says:

> a pluralistic "feast" of ideas is laid out before us—some of it too sweet, too sour, too over-cooked or just plain poisonous, but some of it is subtly flavourful, surprisingly tasty, and good for our hardened arteries. The part sculpture plays in the visual feast is an expansion into all sorts of media and materials ranging from earthworks, site constructions and installations to marked sites, named objects, conceptual performances, and video projections.[4]

Characteristics of Modern Art

Rather than trying to survey these new forms in any detail, I want to suggest that these developments constitute an extremely important moment of opportunity for Christian involvement in the arts. Moreover, however disparate the styles, there are certainly commonalities or tendencies that are important to note. They are not invariably present, but they are increasingly and typically so. Let us review these characteristics and see if they suggest openings for Christian engagement.

An Element of Performance

First, since the initial stirrings of these developments in the work of Jackson Pollock, there has been a growing element of performance in contemporary art. The idea of the artist squirreled away in his or her studio, communing with the gods and then descending from the mountain to deliver the tablets, is gone. Many artists, of course, continue to work in traditional ways, but the art that now captures the attention of people is performed in a more public fashion—or at least has some dimension of performance to it. For many artists, making or mounting the art is at least as important as the object that survives. Even traditional art can be "performed," as when Sister Wendy takes us around the gallery on PBS. But in a larger sense, artists now want to say that meaning in art does not lie in the completed object—or better, it does not lie *only* in that one place. Rather, in an important sense it is created in the experience of making or performing the work. Such a development progressed from taking liberties with the canvas (Pollock), to eliminating the canvas altogether (Allen Kaprow), and finally to creating a visual or dramatic episode out of which meaning or impact is meant to arise (performance art). Often contemporary art seeks to resonate with, even replicate, the dramatic and narrative character of everyday life, and perhaps respond to the contemporary hunger for ritual. This represents an important attempt to reach beyond the work to reconnect what, during the formalist period of modern art, was disconnected: the art and our larger world.

Though this quest is extremely important, it is not altogether new. It resonates with previous periods of art history. This dimension of art recalls the multimedia world of classical opera and before that the medieval sacred dramas. It also embraces in significant ways the developing multimedia world of the late twentieth century. Most importantly, it recalls the dazzling dramatic images of biblical visions of the sacred drama of redemption and the end of history. Surely this development may be creating space for seeing and hearing this larger story "performed." This aspect of art is important for the presentation of Christian truth, for the gospel is not meant only to be seen and heard; it calls for a personal response—for obedience and performance.

An Interactive Character

This leads naturally to a second and more important characteristic of contemporary art. While the traditional categories are breaking down, the possibilities of art are greater than at any time, partly because postmodern art is interactive. Is Andy Warhol's work about painting? Is it sculpture? Or better, is life in Warhol's studio, what was called "The Factory," a kind of performance piece? Are Kaprow's happenings a new form of participatory drama? The common element in these new forms is that they insist on connecting with the viewer, asking him or her to play a role in "completing" the work of art. Meaning is constructed, therefore, out of elements in the artwork but also out of the values and ambitions, the hopes and fears that viewers bring to the work. Artists are not just allowing but often insisting that their work be understood as embedded in some social or political reality. As a result, the reaction of the audience completes the artist's "performance." Again, this characteristic harkens back to previous eras in the history of art. Up until the Renaissance, art was made primarily for devotional purposes. Its entire reason for existing was to play a part in a larger liturgical or devotional setting, to move one to remembrance and prayer. But even more recently, reference to everyday life that became common in the nineteenth century was meant to resonate with common experiences. The viewer was meant to respond to Pablo Picasso's *Guernica* by condemning and perhaps even actively opposing the atrocities of the Spanish Civil War. Art, at its best, is an expression of agency and advocacy; it is meant to provoke and not only to please.

Lynn Aldrich's work illustrates this point well. She takes common elements from everyday life—garden hoses, mothballs, cut-up pieces of cactus—and subtly uncovers the remnants of meaning that inevitably animate these objects. In one installation piece entitled *Bread Line,* she laid a long line of sliced bread across a gallery floor (fig. 25). The aroma of the freshly baked bread filled the space. The presence of the bread, the aroma, and the title of the piece pointed to plenty and want, to abundance and lack, striking deeply into the conscience of viewers (and of critics!). But it is the viewer who has to finish the work. Aldrich simply opened the way to the interaction. As Jude Schwendenwein, a critic writing in *Sculpture* magazine noted, Aldrich "addresses the mortality of all types of matter . . . [and] contemplates the possibility, both literal and spiritual, of running out of nourishment and hence of life itself."[5] But note that this meaning is not resident in the bread itself; it emerges only in relation to the experience the viewer brings—one of hunger or fullness. But like the Dutch still life painters before her, Aldrich insists that the world carries a stubborn meaning that we can bump into but not ignore. "Since I am redeemed, I am at home in the world," Aldrich notes. "The world is a safe place. . . . [People may have] multiple impressions of reality; reality itself is still there within, waiting to be continually revealed by the artist and scientist."[6]

Aldrich's work, incidentally, offers a sharp rebuttal to those who say that since we live in a time when anything goes, no clear witness can be made by a Christian artist. Aldrich wants to say that this is not the case. True, many modern artists tried to close all the doors that led to the supernatural. In one sense, they left us with the object alone. Aldrich answers, all right, let us start with the object and see where it leads. When these objects are placed together carefully, when they are allowed their own voice, they can still speak of human (and even divine) meaning. Even though the other doors are closed, she is saying, creation is such a deep and meaning-filled storehouse that God can come through this door as well as any other.

Fig. 25. *Bread Line,* Lynn Aldrich, 1991, sliced bread, 35¢length. Courtesy of Sandroni Rey Gallery, Venice, California.

Art in its postmodern mode, therefore, frequently reaches across the boundaries of art forms, retrieves meaning from the past, and calls for a response from the viewer. Nicholas Cook, as noted in the last chapter, argues in his discussion of music that artistic meaning, with respect to music, ultimately lies in the experience and not in the notes or even the performance alone. Meaning, if it exists, lies in what the piece does rather than in what it represents. This is true in the visual arts as well. He writes, "The real significance of a painting lies not in the artifact that is hung on the wall, but in the way of seeing the world that it instigates or constructs."[7]

Such a view is well illustrated in the recent furor over the show "Sensation," displayed at the Brooklyn Museum of Art, October 1999 to January 2000. The show included the most recent examples of a new kind of art called Shock Art. Artist Chris Ofili's *Virgin Mary,* for example, was covered with elephant dung. Everyone from Mayor Rudolph Giuliani to President Bill Clinton found it "deeply offensive" (even though most of them hadn't even seen the work). But it turns out that Ofili is a practicing Roman Catholic, and in some African cultures, elephants have totemic power (sometimes linked to the chief) and their dung is sometimes used to make spiritually potent ritual objects. Meanwhile, the exhibit was owned by Charles Saatchi, who had a secret deal with Christie's auction house to (eventually) sell the collection, so commercial interests were also at work. What could better illustrate the way that art is often thrown down like a gauntlet? There you are, the artist is saying. This is my statement. What do you make of it? Since art has in many ways become a part of popular culture, the value of a show, for better or worse, is played out in public reaction and frequently in the interplay of commercial forces. But such is the state of the arts today! Ofili's art is designed not simply to be seen and enjoyed (or even simply rejected). Its central purpose is to continue the older role of the avant garde by shaking deeply held, in some ways even sacred, notions. If this confrontation leads to picketing or media attacks, so much the better. Serious art has once again become a player in contemporary culture.

In the fall of 2000, the Royal Academy in London, scene of the original "Sensation" in 1997, mounted a show called "Apocalypse." Central pieces featured mayhem and horror: Maurizio Cattelan crafted an image of the pope hit by a meteorite, his face twisted with pain; Jake and Dino Chapman created a pile of modeled figures, mutilated and deformed German soldiers perpetrating mass torture on themselves and shoveling bodies into ovens that belched smoke. In his preview of the show, critic Jonathan Jones asked if we are capable of being shocked anymore. The Chapman brothers, when asked, actually laughed at the idea, because their work is intended to morally sidestep something that has become, in their minds, overly cloaked in morality. Jake said of the work, "We would like to think of this as a severely anti-humanist work of art."[8] Are they insisting that any attempted memorial of this horrible event is vacuous? Is this because it is too awful? Or because we cannot judge? Part of the shock may be in the inability to determine the artists' meaning. But, of course, if there were no moral energy or religious sensitivities left in the culture, this art would lose its raison d'être.

The question posed by these exhibits, therefore, is whether anything today can still shock us. The implied answer is yes, for if the answer were no, the artists would not have made the effort. But where can we go to find a basis for our moral outrage? Christians respond that only faith in a holy God can properly ground such outrage. In a sense, these artists are presenting a contemporary morality play, but they are asking for someone to provide the moral of the story. The question is whether Christians are prepared to engage with this challenge.

A Collaborative Character

A related though slightly different characteristic of contemporary art is its collaborative character. If the interactive character spoke of the embrace of the audience as a partner in the artistic process, this aspect speaks of the growing collaboration among artists, between artists and pop culture, and even—to the horror of many supporters of the high arts—between artists and commercial interests. Artists don't rely only on viewers to complete their works. Before the works are viewed, the artists have already embraced influences from many sources. Beginning with the Cubists, who attached pieces of newspapers and books to their work, artists have tended to borrow motifs promiscuously. Robert Rauschenberg is probably the most famous collector of disparate items, but he is certainly not the only one.

Since the Pop artists opened the way, artists have borrowed elements from popular or commercial culture to make ironic references to contemporary life. With the rise of the video and TV culture, a plethora of images became available, along with new media in which to display these images. The use of these media reflects a desire to increase and elaborate the artistic experience to include sounds, visual effects, even kinesthetic effects—as when one walks through Ernesto Neto's tunnel filled with dangling polyp-shaped bags and is invited to pat and push the soft objects. Visual artists seek musicians or visual and dramatic artists to work with in various performance situations. There seems to be a sense in which the arts yearn for such collaboration as though reaching for fuller and richer experiences that incorporate the full sensorium.

Relevant too is the fact that the leading popular arts today are inherently collaborative. Films, TV, even to a certain extent video necessitates artists working with technicians and engineers, or with musicians and writers of various kinds, to say nothing of actors and actresses. The fact that Academy (and Emmy) Awards are still given to individual directors, writers, and actors indicates that artistry can still be recognized and celebrated even when it is exercised in collaboration with others. Artists are often thought of as solitary geniuses who are difficult to work (and live) with, and indeed many no doubt are. But today there seems to be an openness, one might almost say a longing, to work together in making experiences and objects that move and delight audiences.

A further area of collaboration might seem like blasphemy to traditional artists: Much quality art today is made under the auspices of commercial interests. Financial realities are making this necessary, and patronage has for the most part passed from wealthy philanthropists to commercial firms. Even artists in Europe, where government subsidies have been a way of life, are finding these traditional sources dwindling and are finding commercial offers tempting. But are these offers inherently bad? Is art significant only when it is made independently of all such consideratons? More to the point, has art ever been completely independent of such considerations? Certainly, in regard to this, as with any cultural development, the assessment is mixed. Though overriding interest in the bottom line, stock prices, and sales does threaten to predetermine artistic goals and thus can easily prostitute conscientious artists, such considerations are surely not the whole story. Even marketers recognize the value of attractive design in products and advertisements, and these areas are attracting an increasing number of art school graduates. I would even venture to argue that some of the best design work today is being done in these contexts and that this work may well be celebrated in the future as some of the best "art" of this generation.

But as with other contemporary art, creativity in commercial design does not lie only with the artist; it also includes the viewer. Paul Willis, in his important study of youth culture, interviewed a broad spectrum of youth on their reaction to ads. Surprisingly, he found that consumers of ads engage in complex interpretive work; they were by no means passive recipients of these appeals. In fact, he discovered that "they have the capacity to consume commercials independently of the product which is being marketed. Commercials can be cultural products in themselves and consumed for themselves. Thus, the success of any particular commercial is, in this respect, separate from its effectiveness in promoting sales."[9] Clearly, commerical patronage of the arts of all kinds is only going to increase. Many business leaders are developing fresh ethical and environmental sensitivies, and they may well be open to a collaboration with artists that respects the dignity of the art. It certainly makes more sense to engage these opportunities than merely to lament the decline of traditional funding sources.

A final comment on collaboration (and interaction) might be relevant in this context. In Willis's work with British youth, one of his conclusions bears on this conversation in important ways. Most references to "consumer culture," especially in connection with the arts of any kind, tend toward the Chicken Little variety. We are becoming nations of consumers, and art is becoming simply another commodity. Oh my! No doubt there is truth in these worries, and we would be naïve to assume everything in this respect is healthy. But Willis discovered, even among lower-middle-class youth, that there is a significant amount of what he calls symbolic creativity in their choices of products and services. In fact, he argues that work in industrial society has unfortunately become so bureaucratic and impersonal that the creative work people do is often limited to their leisure time. And in this respect, people develop rather sophisticated schemes of symbolic aesthetic standards (what he calls "grounded aesthetics") by which they determine their choices of media and consumer goods. This symbolic creativity, he argues, is actually able to bridge the gap between performance and consumption. Consumers become, as it were, secondary performers actively engaged in building their lives in terms of highly developed aesthetic standards.[10]

Willis's conclusions are suggestive. Often in our discussion of the arts we are hampered by unrecognized assumptions about what passes as real "art" or who is able to appreciate this art. Willis's study suggests that we need to rethink these dichotomies and the elitism that often accompanies our judgments. Artists are increasingly feeling free to adapt and embrace many aspects of popular culture in the service of fine art. Viewers must be invited and enabled to make use of art and symbolic materials in ways that further their own goals. This point will become especially important when we consider the relationship of the contemporary situation to worship life.

A Turn to the Visual

The fourth characteristic of contemporary arts and culture is, if anything, even more controversial. But it is clear by now that postmodern art represents in almost every respect the triumph of the visual and especially moving images. Visual artists up to this generation have been better at dealing with space than with time. As recently as the 1980s Calvin Tomkins could say, "The notion of using video as a purely visual medium seems like a wrong notion to me."[11] Video demands too much attention. "Nothing I have seen to date comes anywhere near justifying those demands." The question was whether artists could learn to control time just as they had space.

Things have moved more rapidly than anyone could have predicted in the 1980s, and the triumph of visual culture is now widely recognized. Video art is featured prominately in the Venice and Whitney Biennials. The generation reaching adulthood today represents the second generation of those raised on TV and videos. They have by all accounts a high sense of visual literacy. I judge that my children "see" probably 50 percent more of a movie than I am able to grasp. This reality is being recognized on every hand, but the debate thus engendered is what to make of it. Is this reality something to celebrate or lament? Christians have tended to come down on the negative side: These developments are a threat to a culture that is centered in the Word. As pointed out earlier, this negativity may have much to do with a lack of tradition in the visual arts and even a fear of the visual that dates back to the Reformation.

Jacques Ellul has probably been the most visible opponent of this turn to the visual. He argues in *The Humiliation of the Word* that this is a potentially disastrous development in that it subordinates the word and its meaning-giving qualities.[12] When sight dominates the ear, he argues, our ability to designate meaning loses out, for the images can demonstrate facts about the world, but they cannot give meaning. Sight situates us, but it makes everything relative to our own point of view.[13] Images call us to a kind of meaningless action in a way that is reminiscent of Ellul's characterization of a deterministic technological society.[14] By contrast, the spoken word involves us in mystery and in drama. Above all, Ellul believes, the word is relational. "Reality apprehended by sight is always unbearable, even when that reality is beauty. We have a horror of reality, perhaps because we depend on it so. Language, even when it is realistic allows us to escape from this terrible reality. Sight locks us up with it and obliges us to look at it." There is no way out—except by controlling and mastering the reality[15]—which is exactly what the technological society does for us. A person can see in a second; hearing takes time,[16] and since it is relational, it calls for exchange. Truth and reality coincide in an image only one time in all of history, in the incarnation—after that they part ways again. He claims:

> The incarnation is the only moment in world history when truth joins reality, when it completely penetrates reality and therefore changes it at its root. The incarnation is the point where reality ceases being a diversion from truth and where truth ceases being the fatal judgment on reality. At this moment the word can be seen. Sight can be believed.[17]

And sight is a foretaste of what is to come in the kingdom of God, but until that kingdom comes, God does not introduce sight into the order of truth![18]

It is difficult to know what to make of this jeremiad. One is sympathetic to Ellul's concern regarding the decline of critical discourse in the traditional sense, and the bewilderment that the visual proliferation causes, even the worry that the visual will diminish the word. These are all necessary concerns. But to assert without further argument that images give us facts without meaning or that only the word is relational does not advance the conversation very far. Do we really have a horror of (visual) reality? The real question, however, is why can't we forge a new alliance between word and image that will help us meet the challenge of this generation? Why did this union of word and image necessarily happen only once, in the incarnation? Does Scripture contain no support for thinking that this event furthered God's purposes with the visual creation, by adding to it "the Word made flesh"?

Neil Postman argues similarly that each medium of communication imposes metaphors that "organize our minds and integrate our experience of the world.

[These] impose [themselves] upon our consciousness and social institutions in myriad forms."[19] The reigning cultural metaphor today is the moving image. "We are now a culture whose information, ideas and epistemology are given form by television, not by the printed word. . . . Print is now merely a residual epistemology, and it will remain so, aided to some extent by the computer, and newspaper and magazines that are made to look like television screens."[20] As a result of this change of metaphor, Postman argues that seriousness, clarity, and value within our public discourse will necessarily suffer.[21] The reason for this, according to Postman, is that a person cannot serve both word and image. But more disturbing for Postman is his assessment that the dominant mode of TV content, trivial entertainment, has become the default mode of dealing with significant issues. In this respect, he analyzes TV news, which lays out all the issues of the world, the trivial and the earthshaking, side by side. But since the news is all given in an "entertainment" format with good cheer on every hand, it provides no grounds to discriminate among these things. The TV is most dangerous, then, not because of its trivialities, which we expect and understand, but because of the things it represents as significant. Each media has an agenda to unfold; it represents a metaphor to unwrap. In a culture defined by a TV metaphor, all subject matter is in danger of becoming entertainment.

Much of Postman's discussion is as relevant as it is highly entertaining. But one puts down the book with a sense of disappointment. Even if everything he says is true, the TV (and videos and movies) are not going to go away any time soon. And in our Christian perspective on God's presence in culture, the media, no less than any other sector, though flawed, still exhibits the common grace of God's presence. Thus, all developments in culture, even when they cannot be simply applauded, can be engaged. We are not doomed to live, as Jacques Barzun has recently argued, through the inevitable decline of civilization.[22] The question is whether the problems are inherent in the medium or in the current commercial arrangements that guide its programming. Are there no constructive ways in which one might engage, as artists and critics, with these reigning media? As Herbert Gans notes, Postman offers no empirical support for his assertions—that public discourse has suffered or that the current reigning metaphor is defective. Indeed, as Gans points out, much of the cultural critique represented by Postman and others is based on a class bias that simply does not like the cultural products that certain people freely prefer and that may in fact further their legitimate interests.[23]

A different perspective on the visual turn is offered by Mitchell Stephens in *The Rise of the Image and the Fall of the Word*. Stephens believes the current revolution will actually give us tools to solve the cultural crisis we are facing. "The moving image has the potential to help resolve our crisis of the spirit."[24] As Postman, Stephens is convinced that the "image is replacing the word as the predominant means of mental transport."[25] But this is an opportunity and not simply a fate: Media are tools by which we can remake the world. Far from discouraging critical thought, therefore, images can be used in a positive way to break the hold of print and linear thinking. This is possible because intepreting images, he believes, requires more imagination, not less.[26] As people grew accustomed to rapidly moving images, they became able to process them more rapidly.[27]

Stephens is clearly a cultural optimist. The growth of visual literacy promises to give humanity the ability it needs to address its problems. The future belongs "to a single, inclusive medium, the one for which humankind has repeatedly demonstrated a preference: video."[28] He is quick to admit, however, that much of what we currently see on video will not accomplish what needs to be done—partly because it is still too dependent on older word-oriented media. We need a complex seeing, and he admits that no impressive examples have emerged yet.[29] But this medium is barely a generation old; we need to give it time. Here Stephens's evolutionary optimism gets the best of him. We surely will not forget narrative discourse, but we will—indeed, we must—venture beyond it, he insists. We need a new kind of logic, consisting of discontinuous peak moments. We must "expect that new ethics and new responsibilities will confront us in the new kinds of relationships that are created among these moments."[30] In the future, he believes, we will shape our arguments more like music than prose, through juxtaposition rather than linear structure.[31] Contrary to what people believe, this video stimulus will perk us up; it will not make us passive. But this is a good thing because "sometime in the twentieth century the print method of analyzing the world began to exhaust itself. . . . Its magic began to run out."[32] In a pointed attack on what we have described as the Protestant imagination, he concludes that print looks from the outside in, but why do we assume there is more truth inside us than out?[33]

Whatever else can be said of such diverse points of view, there is surely a fundamental agreement on all sides that we have entered a visual era. Moreover—though here there is probably less agreement—there is no going back. Whatever cultural critics may think of the current situation, for the most part we cannot turn back the clock. And if we are convinced that Christ continues to be Lord of history, that he is working out his purposes in and through human history, and that he calls us to a glorious future kingdom, we do not want to return to the past. Of course, the world is broken and all developments are tainted with sin and so must be addressed with a great deal of prayer and spiritual discernment, but this was true of previous eras no less than now. We do not endorse the uncritical optimism of Stephens, especially his excitement over the visual replacing and making up for the deficiencies of the verbal. Surely what is called for is a new alliance and interaction between the word and the image. But at least he is right in allowing that these developments, as with modern art generally, may be increasing the ways in which the world can be grasped. We see these developments as ambiguous. There are potential problems, to be sure. If people are raised on images and do not have the skills in manipulating words, they will finally not know the meaning of all they are looking at (here Ellul is right).

But is it not possible to integrate word and image in appropriate and God-honoring ways? Can't the visual be used to add power to the verbal? Clearly, if such a thing is possible, we will need all the imaginative skill our artists can provide.

A Spiritual Element

Finally, postmodern art, with all its collaboration and interaction, often reaches for an experience that is deeply spiritual. I have commented frequently on the turn toward spirituality that marks much recent art. Not that secular prejudice is missing from contemporary art; far from it. Alex Grey, a leading artist who seeks to penetrate into the "soul," recently responded in a letter to a hostile review in the *Los Angeles Times*. The review betrays, he notes, the spiritual blindness of much of contemporary art. "It is my mission to create work that encourages the viewer to see deeply into themselves, into the subtle realms of being, even if such were possible, into their own souls." He wants his art to show the world in its "sacred radiance."[34] Art critic Christopher Knight can even see a spirituality in the new geometric cubism represented by Sol Le Witt. This artist begins with rigorous systems, Knight says, "tight logic and exacting rational thought—and then performs an alchemical transformation. Spiritually exquisite flights of visual imagination emerge."[35] Examples of this spiritual preoccupation could be multiplied.

We can be grateful for these growing sensitivities; indeed, we may even find in their work insights into a spirituality that will challenge our own spiritual perceptions. The problem is that many of these artists have lost touch with the Christian tradition (or even traditions of other religions) that could nourish such sensitivities. Ironically, their handicap may be the reverse of the handicap with which Christian artists today are working. The latter have lost a sense of their own artistic and even imaginative traditions. Just as they have lost their way artistically, their secular counterparts have lost their bearings spiritually. As Christians turn for help to whatever is at hand, their secular neighbors forage through history and cultures for some spiritual orientation. Suzi Gablik has pointed out, postmodern culture is "empty at the center—it has no integrated vision."[36]

Contemporary artists, sometimes consciously, but more often perhaps unconsciously, occasionally stumble upon religious traditions that provide the spiritual nourishment they seek. Recent research has argued that popular music subcultures serve the function of postmodern, quasi-religious communities—these expressions of popular culture, especially rock fesitvals, are in fact a religious phenomenon. Robin Sylvan traces the historical and structural function of these subcommunities (deadheads, hip-hop, raves, and heavy metal) back through African American traditional culture to West African possession rituals.[37] For large groups of music aficionados, the chant put them in touch with religious depths that were missing in their secular lives. Others such as video artist Bill

Viola have sought guidance from Eastern religions. Sometimes an encounter with immigrant religious art and practices moves Americans in deep ways.

Even those of our contemporaries who would call themselves irreligious are not lacking in spiritual sensitivities. As Julian Schnabel noted:

> Duccio and Giotto were painting in a society in which there was actually belief in God. . . . People had religious experiences in front of paintings. The painters were connecting people to something bigger than life, something bigger than their individual experiences. I think people still have religious experiences in front of paintings. The only difference today is that the religion isn't organized or prescribed—it's consciousness. To get religion now is to become conscious, to feel those human feelings.[38]

This expresses well the inward journey of discovery that attracts so many today. Life is a journey in which significance must be collected from various sources, like souvenirs brought home from vacation. But this is not necessarily an individualistic experience. These "faiths" and "moralities" are communally constructed by reference groups we choose and nurture. But the question is whether this spiritual bricolage is able to sustain an imaginative vision large enough to create great works of art. Cultivating a deeper consciousness is good as far as it goes; learning from various traditions is also admirable. But an openness to the sacred, even a deep spiritual hunger, may not be enough to sustain an artistic tradition.

All of this points to the fact that our culture, in the last two hundred years, has lost touch with the religious and mythical traditions that previously provided imaginative vision for artists. It is certainly true that many artists today would argue that this is a good thing—these traditions, in their minds, had become oppressive and obsolete. But it is nevertheless true that the absence of a vital religious center, something that has animated all living cultures throughout history, leaves artists as spiritual orphans. Even the Marxist critic Peter Fuller recognized the gaping hole that the loss of Christianity has left in our worldview.

> Christianity remains a scandal and a stumbling block to the "historical materialist" interpretation of history. It is not just that [these] methodologies have so conspicuously failed to explain why it was Christianity, specifically, which rose to dominance, or how it managed to survive. . . . The problem runs deeper still: the whole question of the historical Jesus, and the beliefs which accrued around him, should cause us . . . to consider just how far we are from understanding the positive role which such great and consoling illusions play in determining man's ethical, cultural and indeed his spiritual life.[39]

But the final word for Christians should be gratitude for the growing openness toward religious traditions, for who can tell when an artist might stumble on a reference that will pique the imagination. The New York artist Makoto Fujimura provides an instructive example. While studying in Japan and rediscovering some of the richness of his spiritual tradition, he found himself open in new ways to the presence of God. One day he came across the last epic poem of William Blake entitled "Jerusalem." Albion in that poem became for him a powerful symbol of all the searching of humanity. At the end of the poem Albion stands at the foot of Christ on the cross, and he stretches out his own arms like Christ and asks:

> "Cannot man exist without mysterious offerings of self for one another? Is this friend-ship and brotherhood?"
>
> Jesus says, "Wouldst thou love one who never died for thee, . . . or ever die for one who had not died for thee? And if God dieth not for Man and giveth not himself eternally for Man, Man could not exist; for Man is Love As God is Love; every kindness to another is a little Death in the Divine Image, nor can Man exist but by Brotherhood."[40]

Fujimura recalls that by the end of the poem he found himself responding to this Christ. "Quietly and unexpectedly, my allegiance shifted from art to Christ."[41]

Interestingly, though his Christian faith was strong and growing, this did not keep him from valuing his own Japanese traditions. He continued his studies in the living and very spiritual tradition of Japanese art. His MFA thesis project (see pl. 4), which has received numerous awards and now hangs in the Museum of the Tokyo National University, combines these two different spiritual influences. In this work, he employs an ancient Japanese technique in the service of his new-found faith, revealing the golden city, "the New Jerusalem, coming down out of heaven from God."[42] Fujimura demonstrates the freedom of the Christian to take what he sees in the contemporary art world and, out of his profound commitments, transform these influences into work that praises God. His work borrows from artists Mark Rothko and Barnett Newman as well as from traditional Japanese art. As he says, "I desire to transform their metaphysical language of abstraction and make the reality of Mary's act of adoration come alive today. In this sense, my work is not abstract; it is a representational depiction of God's Space, His grace arena where we can approach His presence."[43] This account is significant on many levels. First, it suggests ways in which other spiritual traditions can be used and even embraced in the service of an art that is genuinely Christian. But more than this it points to the calling of the Christian to penetrate deeply into the culture of his or her day to discover signs of grace and take them into the program of remaking all things to the glory of God.

Art and the Renewal of Worship

Two Christian artists, Lynn Aldrich and Makoto Fujimura, illustrated ways in which Christians, even in the midst of an artistic world that has lost touch with its Christian heritage, can still find the means to praise God in their work.

Aldrich accepted the constriction that the minimalist tradition imposed on her and found even there, in an elegiac meditation on human artifacts, signs of God's presence. Fujimura, though discovering Christ within the richness of the Christian tradition (in the person of William Blake), was able to use the deeply spiritual traditions of Japanese art to express the reality of his faith. Both have had to make do with the traditions they have inherited; they have not found themselves within a living Christian artistic tradition that could nourish their artistic work. Their work illustrates well the complexity of the current situation in the art world. Contemporary artists have developed surprising spiritual sensitivities, though for the most part they have lost touch with the breadth and depth of the riches of the Christian (or any other religious) tradition. Meanwhile, Christian artists, while often talented and committed, have not been nourished by the riches of a Christian artistic tradition. The one struggles spiritually; the other artistically.

Of course, this is an oversimplification. There are deep spiritual sensitivities among contemporary artists, and many Christian artists are recovering the richness of their heritage. But this way of putting things does point to the double-sided challenge that Christians face: On the one hand, Christians are called to the world, to penetrate it, to become salt and light and find there ways to celebrate the presence of God. Above all they are called to reach out in love and witness to their neighbor. They can do this because this world is never bereft of God's presence and the universal longing for God that is planted in the human heart. On the other hand, Christians are called to grow more deeply into the scriptural and historical traditions of their faith and forge an imaginative vision of the world that reflects the presence of God, and even the splendor of the gospel.

Clearly, the Christian church and Christian artists face an immense challenge, both to reach this generation with the gospel and equally important (and vitally related) to rediscover the imaginative richness of their heritage. Both challenges involve the sensitivities of the visual arts at a deep level. Each is necessary to fulfill the goals of the other: There is no way for the church to interact constructively with contemporary culture without being rooted firmly both in that culture and in the biblical and Christian tradition.

What resources does this Christian tradition give us? As noted in previous chapters, this heritage features a dramatic and history-shaping intervention of God into the world and a living connection between this God and his creation. It features dramatic, even operatic, events that focus on the earth-altering life, death, and exaltation of the God-man Christ. It possesses the libretto of a dazzling finale in which Christ will return in glory and "wipe away every tear from our eyes." Its corporate life focuses on gathering around the preached, sung, and enacted Word and the dramatic reception of the bread and wine.

I would argue that what the developing art world is longing to discover in their multimedia, shock art exuberance is exactly the compelling and integrative experiences that the Christian faith offers. The exciting proliferation of media and styles, the collaborative world-embracing character of contemporary art may have set the stage perfectly for such holistic events; indeed, it has often echoed these events in exciting ways. The world in one sense is ready to see it; perhaps the church is open in new ways to provide it.

While it is true that many Protestant traditions have not formally encouraged the use of art in worship, such a statement calls for qualification. To say that a tradition has not made use of the visual arts is not the same as saying it has no aesthetic tradition or that its worship patterns have no artistic value. Theological traditions always become embodied in particular worship patterns. All that I recommend here, therefore, must be carried out carefully and sensitively in light of these patterns.

Christians in the arts should surely be encouraged to make do in ways that Aldrich and Fujimura illustrate. They illustrate some ways (there are surely many others!) of penetrating and engaging contemporary culture. But the church also needs a growing number of artists who will work more directly in the church setting, who will find ways to connect with biblical patterns of worship. Perhaps we need to develop (or redevelop) the category of biblical spectacle. I am not thinking here necessarily of the Crystal Cathedral variety Easter or Christmas pageants, although some of what happens there is worth noticing. I am thinking instead of a public performance or display that makes use of music, lighting, and visual arrangements to elicit a response. Cyrilla Barr, in an important article on "Music and Spectacle," defines such events as "the literal incarnation of images derived from Scripture, liturgical practices and the exegesis of certain post-Nicene church fathers."[44] It seems to me that such collaborative projects, which could be done on a small or large scale, correspond with both the biblical framework of drama and narrative and with contemporary cultural sensitivities.

Why can't artists, musicians, and technicians participate in creating experiences of worship? Perhaps visual artists, dancers, and musicians could work together to elaborate on the Scripture passage and sermon. Or perhaps visual artists could join with actors to create dramatic pieces that make use of creative lighting and moving images. Most churches have a great deal of talent that could be used to enhance and expand worship, as well as personal and family devotional life.[45]

As with anything else, such projects can be done well or poorly. But who can say it cannot rise to the heights of the classical opera? We will certainly not want to replace the sermon, but we may develop more richly imaginative settings for the sermon (and new formats in which to present it). All this must still include (and not overshadow) the administration of the sacraments, prayer, the reading of Scripture, preaching, and singing. But these, after all, are embodied "performances." Surely if we use the best artistic gifts that a congregation possesses, begin sensitively and wisely—walking before we run—we might develop a vision that can impact the broader world. But this will not happen apart from the renewal of our own spirituality and worship. At the very least the developments in the contemporary arts suggest the possibility for new forms and collaborations that make possible new experiences of worship.

Surely we want above all to be biblical people. In times of transition, the worry about losing biblical truth is understandable. But what does it really mean to speak of worship that is "biblical"? Must it mean only mind-deadening recitals of biblical texts with appeals to the will? Or might it mean performances that in some sense "reflect" and reenact the impact of biblical events? These events, or images, remember, were intended to incite a response on the part of the viewer; they were not to be mere recitations. True, they must be faithful to the biblical account, but there is no reason why they cannot also be artful.

Let us recall here the triangle that Wassily Kandinsky described. He proposed a moving triangle in which the few at the top were pulling the rest of the people toward ever deeper spiritual experiences. We may deplore the theology Kandinsky's vision represents, but is this triangle not characteristic of our church worship experience as well? The pastor is at the top preaching, with performers, choir members, and soloists in between, and the passive "listener" at the bottom. A study of revivals shows that wherever the work of the Spirit creates genuine revival, the triangle is overturned so that those at the "bottom," that is, the whole people of God, are energized and take control of their lives.[46] Conversion and renewal tend to affect the whole of our human lives, not only our wills. Notice that Peter quotes Joel 2:28 when describing what happened when the Spirit came upon the people in the last days. "Your sons and your daughters shall prophesy [preach!], and your young men shall see visions, and your old men shall dream dreams" (Acts 2:17). This sounds like a revival of the imagination to me! When this kind of spiritual renewal takes place, the gifts of God's people are released—one can see it in past histories of revivals, and there are signs of such creativity today. If this can truly happen in our day, there is no telling how exciting our worship can become. We do not need to worry that people will pay attention, for they have a deep and aching hunger for the living God.

making and
looking at art

When it comes to making art, Christians face an opportunity or a challenge, depending on one's perspective. Contemporary art is experiencing unprecedented transitions and tensions. Current uncertainties in the art world have been caused by a variety of factors: Technological developments have made traditional understandings of art obsolete and greatly expanded the possibilities of what the art object (or experience) can be. The market for art is becoming broader and, by the same token, more populist. And the lines between the arts traditionally conceived are growing fuzzy, as is the gap between high and popular art.

Many artists, of course, see this as a time of unprecedented opportunity for the arts. It might present an opportunity for Christians as well—as indeed I have argued it does—except that Protestant churches have lost touch with their heritage in the visual (and certain other) arts and have only recently begun to experiment in this area. Until recently Christians would have discouraged their children from taking up careers in the arts,[1] and as noted, Christian artists have usually not been welcomed into the church. The art world, for its part, while encompassing spiritual sensitivities, retains a good deal of suspicion toward religion, fear of censorship, and a general lack of openness to artistic freedom and experience.[2] Many galleries blatantly refuse to show artists who are openly Christian, though, interestingly, adherents of other faiths—or some generic spirituality—are often welcomed.

Christians, however, possess an incredibly rich biblical tradition—a tradition rooted in a narrative that is punctuated by earthshaking events in which God has revealed himself. Based on its understanding of creation and the incarnation, it is an embodied tradition that celebrates life in this world. Moreover, those caught up in the events of this narrative are called to respond with the whole of their lives and are ultimately moved to song, dance, and drama in the experience of worship. Meanwhile, a growing number of talented artists have a deep Christian faith, even if their relationship to the institutional church is problematic. As professional artists, they are a rich potential resource for the church. Indeed, the depth of perspective they bring, the solidly grounded spirituality, may be just the thing the church needs to connect with an art world that exhibits newly awakened spiritual sensitivities.

Looking at Art: A Christian's Guide

The confused state of contemporary art presents, therefore, either a challenge or an opportunity for Christians, depending on one's perspective. It is to this question of perspective that we now turn. Granted that it is possible for Christians to be involved in the art world—even to do some "good" there—is there any way in which this involvement is truly important? Is it an intrinsic part of our discipleship? Surely, many would argue, it is not as important as the biblical calls to holiness or to make disciples of all nations. But I want to argue that it is not only a critical component of these priorities but an extremely important Christian calling in its own right.

Since I have been involved in the arts in some way for most of my life, I have grown accustomed to fellow Christians responding to my interest with a kind of bemused tolerance. It was ordinarily seen as a hobby, something like stamp collecting or bird-watching—fun and mostly harmless. But Christians usually communicated to me that this was something one might do with one's spare time; such an interest should not consume the central part of life. But I believe this is a dangerous misconception. Even granting the assumption that art is something like a harmless hobby, one might quarrel with the strict dichotomy between hobby and work that is implied. One of the critical functions art may perform is to bring the notion of play back into the center of our lives where it belongs. After all, the morning stars sang together at creation, and the sea monsters played in the sea. Perhaps humans are meant to see their lives as more of a playtime, a dance, or at least a drama. Indeed, it is likely that we would be more productive in our work if we brought a playful spirit into it. Art may help us understand this, and for this reason alone we should think carefully about art. But I will not take the time to pursue this argument further here.[3] I will focus instead on two deeper issues: When we trivialize art, we fail to appreciate the power that our exposure to art inevitably wields, and as a result, we overlook a vital area of potential Christian growth and witness.

The Power of Visual Art and Aesthetic Experience

To see art and the experience of beauty (or ugliness) as incidental to life is to ignore the power that the arts exert on people (even on Christian people).

When the Genesis account at the very beginning notes that "the Lord God made to grow every tree that is pleasant [*hamad*, "desired"] to the sight and good for food" (Gen. 2:9), there is a tacit acknowledgment of the power of visual goodness, either for good or evil. This is underlined in the third chapter when a parallel phrase appears in the temptation narrative: "So when the woman saw that the tree was good for food, and that it was a delight to the eyes . . . she took of its fruit" (3:6). The word study in chapter 3 underlined this power, or "charm" of the visual, and its influence reappears throughout Scripture as capable of either eliciting praise to God or of leading one away from God. The work of our eyes then, biblically speaking, is serious business.

We have seen earlier that the elimination of the visual aspect of our devotion is a result of the lasting heritage of the Reformation. But the seriousness of this fault is increased by the fact that it is so frequently overlooked. Large parts of our visual lives affect us in ways we routinely ignore. T. S. Eliot issues a similar caution with respect to what we read. What we read for profit, for example, our devotional reading, may not influence us as much as what we read for fun. Because the assumptions in the latter books are unnoticed, they seep into our consciousness and strike us deeply. For example, he points out that the narcissism of modern authors is inescapable, especially in what we read for fun. This "individuality" is all moving in the same direction. No one today can escape its currents. The narcissistic image of what it means to be an individual, he says, has become so much a part of our culture that we do not even recognize it as a problem.[4] Similarly, the images of desire or the pursuit of pleasure inherent in our video environment create a certain vision of what it means to be human. This vision exercises a subtle but deep influence on us. What we watch for fun, for pure entertainment, affects us deeply as human beings and must be undertaken, Eliot argues, from a definite theological and ethical standpoint.

In a recent book, Elaine Scarry argues that beauty lies at the basis of all human drives to learn and grow. Arguing from a naturalistic framework, she notes that this is grounded in the fact that the world seems to be shaped in such a way that it welcomes our appreciation of its beauty. She writes:

> At the moment one comes into the presence of something beautiful it greets you. It lifts you away from the neutral background as though coming forward to welcome you—as though the object were designed to "fit" your perception. In its etymology "welcome" means that one comes with the well-wishes or consent of the person or thing already standing on that ground. It is as though the welcoming thing has entered into, and consented to, your being in its midst.[5]

But immediately Scarry faces the problem of accounting for this apparent mutual embrace, since she believes there is no God, no metaphysical reality that endorses this beauty. "[Beautiful things] now seem unable in their solitude to justify or account for the weight of their own beauty. If each calls out for attention that has no destination beyond itself, each seems self-centered, too fragile to support the gravity of our immense regard." She satisfies herself by noting that even without such a transcendent grounding, these experiences lead the perceiver "to a more capacious regard for the world."[6]

If the capacious regard that Scarry calls for is, ultimately, reflective of a Presence lying at the heart of all regard, then for Christians who insist that these aspects of the world speak of the goodness and love of the Creator, such experiences of beauty are intrinsically sacred. (Indeed, I would argue that they are "sacred" both for believers and unbelievers, but I will not pursue this point here.[7]) Something of the loving goodness of God shines through our experience of beauty. This is why we are inevitably moved to put ourselves in the way of such experiences. We deeply long not only for such beauty but, Christians believe, for relationship with the personal presence lying beneath such beauty. As a result, the experience of great beauty often moves unbelievers to seek God, just as it often moves believers to praise, even to song or dance. St. Augustine classically expressed this in his *Confessions:*

> Neither the charm of countryside nor the sweet scents of a garden would soothe (my soul). It found no peace in song or laughter, none in the company of friends at table or in the pleasures of love, none even in books and poetry. . . . These things of beauty would not exist at all unless they come from you. Like the sun, they rise and set. . . . Not all reach old age, but all must die. . . . Let my soul praise you for these things, O God, Creator of them all; but the love of them, we feel through the senses of the body, must not be like glue to bind my soul to them. For they continue on the course that is set for them and leads to their end, and if the soul loves them and wishes to be with them and find its rest in them, it is torn by desires that can destroy it. In these things there is no place to rest, because they do not last.[8]

The power of beauty, then, cannot be ignored, for it is part of the spiritually charged world in which God has placed us.

The Place of Art in Culture

Scarry's book points out another role that art plays. Whether done by Christians or non-Christians, the best art concentrates the values and questions of a particular cultural moment. No one can finish reading Scarry's book and not come away more sensitive, indeed, more deeply moved by the experience of beauty. The book is a kind of handbook of secular spirituality, and it provides a powerful vision of the role beauty plays in our secular and pragmatic culture. Similarly, in the first half of the twentieth century, the bright figures of Henri Matisse, the anguished images of Salvador Dali, even the cubist pictures of Pablo Picasso provided images of war-torn Western culture and its longing for peace, which were conveyed in no other medium.

We noted in the last chapter the turmoil that the nineteenth-century realists introduced into the art world. They felt quite rightly that the power of art should be used to convey values of common people and not simply reflect those of the elite. Their struggle, even though it was not religiously grounded, was an important one that extended well into the next century. Because of the role of the artist at that time, described as avant garde, subsequent generations of artists questioned the suggested answers of the previous generation. They also provoked responses by proposing further intrusions into their art from untapped dimensions of life, often from areas considered popular or common. And their use of such sources reflected their own unique sensitivities. Edouard Manet sought moral grounding in portraying the outcasts of society. Claude Monet found leverage in experimentation with light and color. Vincent van Gogh sought to infuse his quest with real spiritual substance. Paul Cézanne sought the deeper structural (and geometrical) elements of this liberating vision. And so on. One might say that their work represents a continuing conversation about reality and culture. However incomplete each response may have been, together they reflect broad cultural struggles over important values and sensitivities. And subsequent artists often picked up where previous generations had left off. Thomas Crow describes the constructive and positive role this work played in the developing cultural self-understanding:

> Modernist negation . . . proceeds from a productive confusion within the normal hierarchy of cultural prestige. Advanced artists repeatedly make unsettling equations between high and low which dislocate the apparently fixed terms into new and persuasive configurations. . . . [These were] as productive for affirmative culture as they are for the articulation of critical consciousness.[9]

Consider how Edgar Degas embraced the world of dancers, how the cubists included in their paintings bits and pieces from ordinary life, or the way in which Salvador Dali used dream images. Each of these artists in his own way disturbed the traditional rules of acceptable subject matter but in so doing extended the range of art's critical conversation.

To ignore these voices, therefore, is to deprive ourselves of data critical to understanding and appreciating cultural values and questions. These voices reflect, we believe, the operation of common grace. That is, God's presence is evident not only in the church or among Christians but also more broadly in culture through those most gifted and sensitive to the nature of things. Just as we would be foolish to ignore discoveries of science just because they were made by non-Christians, so we would be foolish to ignore cultural voices when it is clear that they speak honestly and, within their context, truly. We believe we have something to share with these neighbors, but we also have much to learn from them. The depth and richness of our lives are diminished when we ignore their voices.

Precisely because the arts are a critical kind of cultural compass, they must not be ignored by Christians who seek to answer the call to witness and praise. The views of Scarry and Augustine quoted earlier illustrate this point: To neglect art is to overlook a critical means of bringing outsiders to Christ (as well as facilitating our own praise). The experience of art, precisely because it ultimately refers to God, can be a preparation for faith, an enlargement of spiritual vision. This fits well with C. S. Lewis's argument in *An Experiment in Criticism*. There he argues that in learning the skill of interpreting and understanding works of art (what is called "criticism"), we seek an enlargement of our being through a shared vision with the artist. In such experiences, we are able to get beyond ourselves and see with different eyes. Because, Lewis says, "My own eyes are not enough for me, I will see through those of others. I am never more myself than when I do."[10]

Experiencing a work of visual art is meant to focus our attention on one place for one moment of time, in a sense allowing us to see all of life in that one moment. Like the biblical notion of Sabbath (which means at its root to "stop"), art stops us in our tracks and forces us to pay attention to life in a way that we have not previously done. The painting that arrests our gaze in the gallery insists that we ignore all the needs and duties of everyday life and look at life, as it were, from a distance. Unlike music, which plunges us into time and holds us there until it brings its harmonic world to resolution, visual art stops time. In such experiences, art provides an important image of transcendence with which Scarry and many others have wrestled. But for Christians it is a transcendence that points us, indeed, can help connect us, to the personal ground and meaning that is God. This experience for the Christian is grounded in the fact that God himself has become part of the creation in Jesus Christ, and as we are rooted and grounded in Christ, the power of the Holy Spirit enables us to shape lives (and materials) in ways that bring glory to God. As John Navone puts this, "True beauty as attractiveness of the truly good motivates human life and development in that intellectual, moral and religious self-transcendence that constitutes human authenticity."[11]

But the experience of art also provides an image or echo of redemption as well. The artist always starts with something in the world—objects, colors, shapes—and collects and draws out the "sense" that the Creator has placed in these things, and shapes this into an image of meaning. This process implies that the world need not be left as it is; it is "redeemable." Of course, we believe that the world is subject to this "redemptive wish" because of who God is and what he has done with the world.[12] The Christian believes God, in Christ, has taken on the reality of the creature and continues to indwell it by the Holy Spirit, working in it to embrace all things within the tapestry of praise in the new heaven and new earth. God, in other words, has created the world susceptible to transformation. And as he works in it his gracious purposes that come to focus in Jesus Christ, so we—Christians or not—may work in the direction of these purposes. God by the Spirit indwells both the time of the musician and the space of the artist.

Why is thinking about art in this way difficult? The reasons are many, but two are especially important. First, culture and education have taught us to see the world on its own terms—that is, without reference to God or the supernatural. Even Christians frequently forget how to connect the depths of their experience with God. They are often afflicted with the gnostic temptation to split off God and his purposes from their everyday world. So they enjoy the world, even thank God for it, but they cannot see how God is present in their experiences of the world.

A second reason why Christians have difficulty connecting art with godliness also grows out of the disenchantment of the world. We have been taught to believe that art, if it has value, needs to be explained (often explained away) in terms that are clearly related to scriptural truth. Consider the way standard Bible study materials seek to help the reader understand the true meaning of the many biblical images, usually by putting them in an outline or visual chart. There is the fear that if we do not understand some image or picture rationally—what is sometimes called "biblically"—we will miss what it is saying. But images have their own impact to make that can affect us deeply and draw us closer to God or move us away.

We overlook this potential because we are more at home with words than with images. Recently, during a worship service I attended, some reproductions of Rembrandt's works were displayed on a screen while Baroque music played—the music and the art wonderfully underlining the content of the service and its Easter theme. Afterward I overheard someone comment that he saw no need in showing the pictures; there was no value added in the art. In his mind, the art added nothing to the music and the sermon.

We have noted some of the historical reasons for this lack of imagination, but there is also an important philosophical reason for it. Because of our Platonic heritage, we privilege the invisible (and cognitive) over the visible, or to put it another way, we privilege meaning over form. But this is precisely what the Christian doctrines of creation and incarnation should make impossible. God the eternal Creator became flesh and dwelt among us, John says, and we "have seen his glory" (John 1:14). Notice that it does not say we understood his glory; indeed, in many ways we do not and will not really understand it—at least until our eyes are finally opened in heaven. But here and now we are enabled to behold in some ways the glory of the Lord—we do see even if, Paul notes, it is through a glass darkly. One day we will see face to face; which is to say we will know fully as we are known by God (1 Cor. 13:12).

As mentioned earlier, Mitchell Stephens argues that we live in an increasingly visual world. This means, like it or not, we must come to terms with the visual in a way that we have not had to do previously. This means recovering a more robust sense of the goodness of the material and the visual. In doing so we are only echoing God's judgment that all the material things he has made, the feldspar as well as the nuthatch, are very good. This is not to say, of course, that the visible is more important than the invisible, the image preferred to the word. Clearly this would be an overreaction to past mistakes, for apart from the revealed (verbal) description of the glory of Christ, we would have no understanding of what it is Christ came to do. A crucifix, however moving it might be as art, would have less meaning (and therefore less impact) were it not for the biblical testimony that this event was "for our sins," or for "the ministry of reconciliation." Art, therefore, just as biblical imagery, must be experienced holistically, in ways that integrate intellectual, visual, and emotional elements.

The Place and Importance of Art Criticism

Art is an intentional practice that demands patience and application both on the part of the artist and the viewer. Therefore, critics and teachers can help us see a work of art, which cannot simply be "explained," more clearly. Like any other cultural activity, looking at art is an activity that takes time and patience. And in this process there is a proper and potentially important role that an art critic can play. Criticism, like any cultural practice, can be a good thing or a bad thing. We have already described what it shouldn't do: It should not stand in the way of the work. The proper work of a critic is, in the first instance, not to judge a work but to remove obstacles to better enable a viewer to see what is really there. We have pointed out that Christian discussion of art often errs by explaining (or sometimes deconstructing) a work of art in too narrowly Christian terms. Of course, secular commentators are sometimes similarly eager to provide explanations that are clearly mistaken. In both cases, explanations stand in the way of the work rather than shed light on it.

I once heard a museum docent describe a Dutch still life in a lecture. She pointed out the flowers that held snails and beetles, which for seventeenth-century Dutch people were natural symbols of vanity and the brokenness of creation, reminding them that life is always involved with death. She then went on to note how this demonstrated the Dutch painters' need to "moralize" about life through their paintings. Quite apart from her strange use of "moralizing"— would she have felt Picasso was "moralizing" in his painting *Guernica*?—this was simply not true. Dutch painters felt no such need. They simply observed that the world included snails and beetles and that even beautiful flowers could not be properly understood without reference to such things. They felt this juxtaposition portrayed the way things actually were in the world, not how they would like them to be. While it is true that they connected such things to their religious views, their perspective is certainly not forced on the viewer through their still lifes. The painters simply assumed the meaning of things (and thus the morality) was built in, not imposed. Indeed, one might argue that nineteenth-century painters of flower pieces were more truly moralizing because they painted the world as they wished it were—without beetles and snails—rather than as it actually was. Such explanations stand in the way of understanding because they say more about the critic than they do about the work of art; they distract one from what is obviously there.

This point may be made even clearer by referring to the analogous role biblical commentaries play in our understanding of Scripture. Commentaries should not stand between the text and the reader; rather, they should open up the text, enhancing the reader's own experience. Just as commentaries are best read in the light of one's own firsthand experience with Scripture, criticism must be read and applied in the light of our own careful and thoughtful openness to the work of art. We must stop long enough in its presence to allow it to work on us, bringing all our critical faculties and especially our understanding of the presence of God to the experience. In this way, art can become a natural extension of our prayer and devotional life.

The Question of Censorship

At this point someone will want to raise an objection. Surely a certain amount of the art we might look at today will not only *not* contribute to spiritual growth but may actually impede it. How can a Christian remain pure in the midst of the filth that goes by the name of art and culture? This is a fair question, especially given that some of the more visible currents of contemporary art intentionally flout accepted standards of morality, even decency. Especially in light of the claim that art can draw us to God or move us away, the question of what we should allow ourselves to see deserves serious attention.

Let me address this by making two foundational claims.[13] While the above question is a fair question, I do not think it is the first one Christians should ask. Regarding many areas of the Christian's life, the New Testament makes it clear that the first question is not, What evil should I avoid? The more important question is, What good should I pursue? In fact, Paul is noticeably cool toward those who would make rules about what not to taste or touch or handle. In one place he goes so far as to say, "These [regulations] have indeed an appearance of wisdom in promoting self-imposed piety, [and] humility . . . but they are of no value in checking self-indulgence" (Col. 2:23). In other words, even if we could come up with a set of rules concerning what to avoid looking at, these rules in themselves would not go far toward promoting holiness.

The more fundamental question then is, What good should I pursue? The New Testament does provide some solid advice regarding this question. Paul often says things such as seek peace, pursue what is good, learn to discern what is of value. In the clearest passage along this line, Paul advises us not to worry about anything, but to "let your requests be made known to God" (Phil. 4:6). Having committed to God our concerns, no small thing in itself, we are free (liberated) to focus on the things that are honorable, just, pleasing, excellent, and praiseworthy. He summarizes: "If there is any excellence and if there is anything worthy of praise, think about [reflect on] these things" (Phil. 4:8). Interestingly, he goes on to say, keep on doing all the things that you have learned and received from me, "and the God of peace will be with you" (v. 9). Goodness, in other words, is meant to be practiced (not just considered), and, Paul implies, when it is, you will know God's peace (see vv. 7, 9).

But, you say, holding to what is good is a general rule that oversimplifies a complex situation. One cannot look only at the "good"; indeed, it is impossible to learn about the good apart from an engaged process of sorting and evaluating. This inevitably involves exposure to a fairly wide variety of art and an investigation of things that turn out to be inferior. But this positive guideline is helpful because it is often easier to recognize what is worthy than to understand the second rate or harmful, especially when our time and energies are limited. Spend your time with the former, Paul advises; don't worry about the latter. This strikes me as a variation of Christ's advice to seek first the kingdom of God (Matt. 6:33), and those other worries will take care of themselves. As with any cultural practice, gradually one will begin to discern what is better and will be drawn to "approve what is good." In the end, in other words, we will discover that the biblical guidelines are sound.

A second claim relates to this. The basic attitude of a Christian should not be one of worry—Have I done enough? Am I doing the right thing? Have I made a blunder?—but one of confidence and hope. "I am convinced," Paul says boldly, "that neither death, nor life, nor angels, nor rulers, nor things present, nor things to come, nor powers, nor height, nor depth, nor anything else in all creation, will be able to separate us from the love of God in Christ Jesus our Lord" (Rom. 8:38–39). While there was evil on every hand, nothing Paul encountered in this life, he believed, could separate him from God. Remember, Paul tells Timothy, God "did not give us a spirit of cowardice, but rather a spirit of power and of love and of self-discipline" (2 Tim. 1:7). Not that there is nothing in the world to fear—the devil does go about as a roaring lion, Peter says—but our first thought is one of confidence that we belong to God, not fear of what the devil might do. By his death and resurrection, moreover, Christ has been made Lord over all of culture, and one day every knee shall bow before his lordship.

Christians, of course, cannot escape the reality of evil in the world, even if they wanted to. As people who are also subject to the suffering and sin that characterize a fallen order, we cannot always look away or live in denial of evil. We are called to discipleship in the middle of this suffering world, not somewhere on the edges where we might feel safe. And since art inevitably reflects this fallen order, even—or we should say, especially—good art will include elements that are ugly, painful, or erotic. These are part of the truth about reality that is the raw material of artistic production. Indeed, I believe we can go far-ther. It is sometimes in an encounter with the darkest art that we are challenged to rethink some of our glib conclusions. It may be when we see the human sit-uation at its most hopeless that we can see more clearly how hope is constructed (or lost).

This all implies that discernment is not a matter of rules—always keep from this or that. Nor is it blanket permission to do what you please—this would deny the spirituality of art and imply, mistakenly, that art is simply a harmless hobby. Discernment is rather a skill that is learned over time and that varies from culture to culture. Moreover, it is a process that is learned and practiced in community, for it is together as the body of Christ that we come to under-stand what is good and what is not. If we feel the viewing of certain things is appropriate but no one else in our fellowship feels that way, we have good rea-son to rethink our attitude, or at least to listen carefully. It is in corporate dis-cussion and prayer that we come to "discern what is good."

Above all, bear in mind that gaining discernment is a part of the larger process of becoming like Christ. Here Scripture, prayer, and mutual admonition all play a critical role. A summary of these musings might be: Stay close to your broth-ers and sisters as you, together, stay close to Christ. When we love Christ whole-heartedly, the experience of art—whether making or viewing—can surely become a part of that process by which we grow up into him in all things (Eph. 4:15).

The Relationship of Beauty to Goodness (and to God)

A critical question in this day of economic inequality and the cultivation of marginalized voices involves the relationship between art and the quest for political justice. Christians often find themselves asking, Do the pursuits of jus-tice and beauty compete for our attention, or do they converge in some way? How can I enjoy quiet moments of beauty when the world is full of suffering? Interestingly, this is not a question that only Christians ask; it is also a hotly debated issue in secular universities. In these settings, there has been a reaction against the study of English as a dispassionate pursuit of truth and beauty, often expressed by groups previously marginalized in the university—women and minorities. These groups see the study of art and literature as necessarily sub-ordinated to their pursuit of justice.

Christians, of course, have similar concerns. The friends I mentioned ear-lier who could not see the value of my interest in art most likely held their views in the name of a certain hierarchy of spiritual values. This hierarchy would have been expressed roughly as follows: Things such as art (or gardening, or hiking, or waterskiing), while certainly not harmful, are not as important as, say, preach-ing the gospel, or pursuing holiness in one's life, or feeding the homeless. In a sense, we have dealt with the first two of these supposed priorities (preaching and holiness) in noting our philosophical predilection for the "spiritual" (read invisible) over the "physical," which, I argued, more likely derives from Plato than from Paul. But issues of justice and art are more troubling. At first glance, at least, the charge that a concern for beauty should be subordinated to a concern for the poor seems persuasive. Don't we believe after all that people are more important than things, and therefore, a concern for their well-being must take precedence over a concern for well-wrought objects or events?

This debate between goodness or justice and beauty is a central concern of Elaine Scarry's book *On Beauty and Being Just*. She notes that recently the political argument against beauty has been voiced in the university as a response to unjust social arrangements. A preoccupation with beauty distracts one, according to this argument, from efforts to bring about a more just social situation. But Scarry believes such prioritization is mistaken. On the contrary, she argues, the uneven aesthetic surfaces of the world themselves exert a pressure toward social equality. This pressure, she notes, results from the symmetry that is essential to beauty (and that models a kind of social symmetry); it comes from the pressure exerted against "lateral disregard," that is, the failure to look lovingly and sensitively not only at beautiful things but also at things that lie around this beauty; finally it comes from the sensitized perceptions that the pursuit of beauty elicits. According to this view, exercising one's taste for beauty activates sensitivities that also oppose injustice.[14]

But she admits, even if the idea of ethical fairness comes to mind at the moment one looks at beauty, it remains abstract. Nothing actually requires us to work toward the enactment of social symmetry. Here, Scarry notes, we are helped by listening to Simone Weil, the mystic who died working for justice in a German concentration camp.[15] At the point we see something beautiful, Weil argues, we experience a radical de-centering. Beauty, according to Weil, requires us to "give up our imaginary position at the center. . . . A transformation then takes place at the very roots of our sensibility, in our immediate reception of sense impressions and psychological impressions."[16]

Weil is arguing, according to Scarry, that the experience of beauty forces us to get ourselves out of the way, as it were. Therefore, this experience itself helps prepare us to work on behalf of others. But while this may be true, it is not exactly the thrust of Weil's argument. Weil, who was well known as a Christian mystic, is not saying that beauty by itself requires us to give up our position at the center. This is something that God requires. She argues, in the passage to which Scarry refers, that the love of beauty is the complement of the love of our neighbor. These both "proceed from the same renunciation, the renunciation that is an image of the creative renunciation of God."[17] So it is not beauty but God who has "conferred upon [humanity] an imaginary likeness of this power, an imaginary divinity, so that [we] also, although a creature, may empty [ourselves of our] divinity." It is "God who provides us with a model of the operation which should transform all our soul" and enables us to undergo this radical decentering. And in the part of Weil's reference that Scarry pointedly leaves out, renouncing ourselves "not only intellectually but in the imaginative part of our soul . . . means to awaken to what is real and eternal, to see the true light and hear the true silence," which is God.[18] The experience of beauty and goodness are related, therefore, but not, as Scarry argues, at the level of perceptual practices alone. They are related because both have their ground in God. And to insist on this relationship, as Scarry does, without the ground in which this relationship stands, is to misconstrue the nature of our situation.

This grounded relationship that Weil argues for fits well with the biblical views of beauty and goodness we considered earlier. Throughout Scripture, words for goodness and beauty overlap, and their realities are often indistinguishable because they both express God's own goodness and his integrated purposes for creation. When God said of creation, "It is very good," was he making an ethical judgment? An aesthetic one? Clearly he intended both. And it is true, as Scarry argues, that injustice is a kind of ugliness. In Scripture, beauty, when it is taken out of its context in goodness, becomes a snare, even an abomination to God. It is only from the perspective of God's purposes for creation and his redemptive strategies that one can see clearly to make these judgments. But beyond making judgments, those decentered by God's transforming work are called to a life of sacrificial service both toward the created order and especially toward those who bear the image of God. Even as both visual splendor and substantial goodness are rooted in God, so pursuit of both values belongs to the call of the Christian. It is to a further elaboration of this assertion that we now turn.

Does Art Play a Role in Discipleship?

In what terms can we specify the role of the arts in discipleship? We have spoken about art's general dependence on creation and even on God's presence there. But how does this dependence work its way into the lives of artists (or art lovers)? If what we are saying is true, there is a sense in which being an artist and being a Christian is related. One can be a Christian and not be an artist, certainly, but being a Christian and an artist ought to make it easier to understand what Christianity is at its core. Madeleine L'Engle puts this even more strongly: "Almost every definition I find of being a Christian is also a definition of being an artist."[19]

The first way in which art and discipleship are related is found in the nature of servanthood. One of the most potent symbols that Christ applied to himself was that of the Servant of the Lord, an image taken from the Servant Songs in the Book of Isaiah. At a critical point in Jesus' ministry, in spite of the crowds that followed him, he ordered them not to make him known. Matthew goes on to say, "This was to fulfill what had been spoken through the prophet Isaiah: 'Here is my servant, whom I have chosen, my beloved, with whom my soul is well pleased. I will put my Spirit upon him, and he will proclaim justice to the Gentiles. He will not wrangle or cry aloud, nor will anyone hear his voice in the streets'" (Matt. 12:17–19). Later Jesus gave further substance to this image when he described the character of his servanthood. His disciples frequently discussed what their discipleship would earn them in terms of worldly power when Jesus finally announced his kingdom. In Mark 10 Jesus tells them it will not be what they expect. Greatness in his kingdom has to do with servanthood. "Whoever wishes to be first among you must be slave of all. For the Son of Man came not to be served but to serve, and to give his life a ransom for many" (Mark 10:44–45).

To be sure, Jesus' servanthood was unique, but the New Testament is clear that we should, both in mind and manner, model ourselves after him. Because of what he was, God's servant, servanthood has taken on a new meaning. This meaning relates to Christians, of course, but it resonates in a special way with artists, for artists are called in a particular way to serve the created order. However creative they are, they can do nothing without making careful use of the sights and sounds into which they are born. All of us are embedded in this created order, according to Genesis 1, and we are called to have dominion over it, but this dominion is further defined in Genesis 2:15 in a way that has special relevance to artists. The man and the woman are to watch over the created order and care for it. However easily most people can forget this basic calling—especially with the ease of modern life—the artist cannot. Mathematicians and philosophers may live with ideas; the artist cannot live without the world of nighthawks and maple trees. Georges Rouault used to say that there is a child in every artist who treasures every object. He used to love to walk along strange streets while on vacation, pausing to peer intently into store windows, stopping to pick up discarded paper on the street. He was a servant of his physical environment. Touch, taste, sight, sound—through these senses the artist hears the call to servanthood. Artists serve by responding and collecting the most characteristic samples. In the person creation speaks; and a person speaks only in creation.

But there is also suffering. Artists are servants who must suffer at the hands of the creature. Christ put this in the starkest terms: "If any want to become my followers, let them deny themselves and take up their cross and follow me" (Matt. 16:24). Again this is a call to all Christians, but artists understand this call, it seems to me, in a particularly intimate way. Artists are called to suffer in and with the material they handle. Making art is a daily discipline. One must spend time in reflection and prayer, though this is not the whole of the Christian life. Similarly, one may spend time in reflection, but that is not art. Art is after all largely a craft, a sitting down to work with materials. And here the pain (and the joy) begins, for immediately the recalcitrance of the materials confronts the artist. Since I work with words, I understand best the feeling of utter dismay at the slipperiness of words, their fragility, their inability to bear all that I want to put on them. I know with T. S. Eliot that "Words, strain/Crack and sometimes break, . . . /Will not stay still.[20]

But there is no shortcut. As Nicholas Wolterstorff put it, we must be led along in conversation with our materials, for the materials must carry the sense if it is to be carried at all. Meaning must somehow be coaxed out of the paint tube or the pencil.[21] Vincent van Gogh (1853–1890) understood this as well as any artist:

> At the moment I am absorbed in the blooming fruit trees, pink peach trees, yellow white pear trees. My brush stroke has no system at all. I hit the canvas with irregular touches of the brush, which I leave as they are. Patches of thickly laid-on color, spots of canvas left uncovered, here and there portions that are left absolutely unfinished, repetitions, savageries; in short, I am inclined to think that the results are disquieting and irritating as to be a godsend to those people who have fixed preconceived ideas about technique.[22]

There is simply no substitute for the anguish or drudgery of this conversation with the materials. We work through and with sketches, outlines, notes, scraps of drawing, or color. Making is practice. And like discipleship, it is an obedience, a doing, and in this work the Christian is carrying out his or her obedience—this is the cross the artist is asked to carry.

This brings us to an even deeper analogy between the work of making art and following Christ, for there is a mysterious dimension to this conversation with materials. In a real sense, as the artist becomes possessed with the process, as van Gogh was, the material, the work, takes on a life of its own, and the artist loses a sense of his or her separate identity. There is a death. Almost in exactly the terms Jesus put it: "Those who find their life will lose it, and those who lose their life for my sake will find it" (Matt. 10:39). Great artists often speak of not having ideas but of being possessed by them. At certain points, they speak of losing a sense of what is happening so that the work can live on its own. After all, the anguish and discipline of art is not born until the artist reaches the point where the work becomes the most important thing—until the artist is willing to give himself or herself over to the work so that it can take on a life of its own. Madeleine L'Engle described this process: "Great artists dying to self in their work, collaborate with their work, know it and are known by it as Adam knew Eve and so share in the mighty act of creation."[23]

But after the death there is often the great joy of discovery. By giving themselves up, artists, not always but occasionally, find that something new is born. Though this may seem incredible to most, the artist understands it well—it is inherent in the nature of discovery and making. Could this be because the act of making art is a reflection of a greater order of things, which the Bible describes as dying to live? Is it a reflection of a life that is given up, through discipline and sometimes through suffering, to serve God and neighbor? Of course, the practice of art in one sense is nothing like the cross Christ bore, but it is a particularly demanding discipline—it requires sacrifice. Moreover, this is a life that all Christians are called to live, and I would argue that in a certain way living such a life is always creative—whether one is an artist, a farmer, or a lawyer. Heeding the strange-sounding call to give up our life to find it, we can then better understand Paul's insistence: "We do not proclaim ourselves; we proclaim Jesus Christ as Lord and ourselves as your slaves for Jesus' sake" (2 Cor. 4:5). Artists are not able to live such a life any easier than anyone else, but they should be the first to understand the basic structure of such a life. It resonates with their special vocation, for without this servanthood of suffering and death, nothing new is made. Christian artists, for their part, may have a particularly important role in showing that there is still something, or Someone, worth dying for.

conclusion

Dreaming Dreams and Seeing Visions

Something is going on in Christian churches, and fascinating changes are taking place in the art world. What does it all mean? From one point of view, it is difficult to be optimistic about prospects for the church: We see around us continuing decline in mainline denominations, widespread cultural apathy toward institutions in general and churches in particular, and a spiritually demanding younger generation. And yet, even as secular commentators recognize, in many places (especially in our threatened cities) the church is one of the few remaining communities on which the health of any society depends. With all its flaws, the church can mobilize and inspire people as can no other contemporary organization—in a way neither the government nor the school system can do. Most importantly, the church holds in its hands the treasure of the gospel—that world-transforming story of God's creative and redemptive work in Christ through the power of the Holy Spirit. This keeps us from despair and gives us hope.

But this hope, I have argued in this book, must include a broadening of vision and of imagination. It must involve, somehow, taking the gospel deeper into our singing, walking, and working—into that deepest part of ourselves where our hopes and ambitions lie. This means also that Christians must discover a renewed vision for the arts, especially the visual arts—a "renewed vision" because the gifts of imagination and vision are a part of the Christian's birthright that is frequently overlooked. But the recovery of an artistic imagination cannot be separated from the renewal of the faith of God's people; in fact, these renewals are intimately related. We need a threefold renewal: a new vision for the arts, a renewal of the worshiping life of the church, and a restored tradition of Christian art.

155

A New Vision for the Arts

God's people need to recover their visual imagination. As noted, there are many reasons for our present situation. The most pressing factor is the changing cultural situation in which we find ourselves. Culture has made a turn toward the visual, and with the rise of new media, the visual image has come to occupy an unprecedented central place in our lives. Someone calculated that a Puritan in early America listened to an average of five thousand sermons in his or her lifetime; an American growing up today will watch at least seven thousand TV programs and a couple thousand movies in his or her lifetime. While the world of our forefathers and mothers was mediated to them through the preached Word, ours is interpreted in terms of images. We noted the ambiguous character of these developments. When images come without verbal context and interpretation, they may, critics argue, discourage critical thinking and analysis. But there is also evidence that such images can stimulate a new visual literacy and imaginative potential.

Christians should not play the visual against the verbal. For Christians, who are people of the Book, the verbal revelation of God's Word will always have unique authority. But we also noted the important role the visual played in Scripture and, obviously, in God's purposes for his creatures. In an earlier chapter, we reviewed the biblical grounds for affirming the visual as theologically significant. God lovingly fashioned a creation that sparkles with signals of his transcendence, and he in fact entered into the creature's depths in Christ and began there the process of transformation from within. The temple, the visions of the prophets, the spectacle of Pentecost, and the vision on Patmos all serve as precedents to encourage Christians to exercise a sanctified visual imagination. They even give us warrant to claim the stimulus of the Holy Spirit for the project.

There are no adequate grounds to resist this turn to the visual—no reason to believe the visual is inherently bad. Theologically, though all cultural trends, as all people, are flawed, they are also redeemable. Through the presence of the Spirit, God works in culture through what is called common grace. On historical grounds, moreover, there are reasons to applaud these developments. The Christian faith, throughout most of its history, was conveyed at least as adequately through its buildings and images as through its theological texts. These visible forms sometimes provided a more striking interpretation of Scripture than the texts of theologians—they were certainly more accessible to people. Indeed, these "media" were only rarely, during Christianity's iconoclastic periods, seen as being in competition with each other. They were rather seen as complementary. Why can we not recover this wholesome synergy?

So while it offers special challenges for the Christian, the turn toward the visual, on the part of our culture, rests on a sound instinct. It reflects the fact that we are creatures of space and time. It suggests that the arts, even the popular arts, have intrinsic attraction. If we are to be citizens of this time, we must learn to speak (and enjoy) this visual language, even as we seek to translate the gospel into its colors and tones.

Renewed Faith and Worship

Claiming the stimulus of the Holy Spirit is not an optional accessory of the Christian life, and any artistic renewal in and for the church can come only in connection with a renewal of congregational faith and worship. Again there are good historical grounds, stretching back into Scripture itself, for making this particular claim. Each time the Spirit moved among the people of God, there was a cultural renewal: People rediscovered their own potential and often dreamed of new forms of life and community—insights that, arguably, stand at the heart of Western civilization. Not infrequently this led to new imaginative and artistic visions of life and the world. This, after all, is what Joel promised and what Peter insisted was happening in Acts 2:17–18:

> In the last days it will be, God declares,
>   that I will pour out my Spirit upon all flesh,
>   and your sons and your daughters shall prophesy,
>   and your young men shall see visions,
>   and your old men shall dream dreams.
> Even upon my slaves, both men and women,
>   in those days I will pour out my Spirit;
>   and they shall prophesy.

Notice in particular how this promise includes those who, in that culture, would be least expected to receive dreams and visions: daughters, slaves, women, all flesh. The triangle of giftedness, which Wassily Kandinsky proposed, will be overturned. No longer will the few gifted ones lead the way; everyone will be special recipients of the gifts of the Spirit—the imaginative worlds will be open to all. There is no indication in the text that this democratization of the Spirit would not have a continuing reality nor that it could not be experienced afresh today.

More importantly, there are signs that the contemporary renewal of worship is accompanied by a fresh understanding of God's presence and working. Many people are recognizing, in James Torrance's words, that "worship is the gift of participating through the Spirit in the incarnate Son's communion with the Father."[1] They are realizing that worship reflects the loving relationships within God and issues in a life of restored relationships—with God, each other, and the created order. This restoration enables us to live a life that, in all its dimensions, glorifies God. Hughes Olds insists that this calling to live our lives to

God's glory is intrinsic to true worship. "The ultimate place in which we must search for meaning of worship is in God's calling us to live to the praise of his glory, his creating us to serve him."[2] These writers and others have contributed to a deeper understanding of biblical worship, which internally reflects and grows out of the presence and activity of the Trinity and externally leads to a renewal of life that reflects this divine reality. The implications of this theological reality for those with special artistic gifts are, if anything, more far-reaching than for others in the body of Christ.

We have noted that a renewal of worship inevitably accompanies a fresh working of God's Spirit. As the Book of Acts shows, such renewal is not always peaceful. Indeed, worship life during periods of renewal is often downright unruly; such periods certainly upset traditional forms. There is ample evidence of this in contemporary worship. Consider the raucous development of Pentecostalism during the twentieth century and the "excesses" it was accused of! And yet it is difficult to envision the worship life of the average renewed church at the beginning of the twenty-first century apart from this charismatic influence. Consider the proliferation of "Independent" churches in Africa and Latin America, with their strange practices and dress. Yet the vitality of the African and Latin American church is sure to be one of the greatest events in the coming century and will not be without its influence on the worship of the church worldwide.

What is interesting to observe is the way these renewals are often accompanied by a fresh use of visual media. The Pentecostal churches early in the last century produced colorful banners, which they carried in their services. The renewal in the Catholic Church, growing out of Vatican II (1961–1965), has included a proliferation of superb visual art. Catholic artist Georges Rouault (1871–1958), whose work was deeply Christian, worked for most of his life without any notice of the Catholic hierarchy. But since the 1960s he has become widely appreciated in the church. Graham Sutherland (1903–1980), who was recognized as one of the leading figurative artists in Britain during the twentieth century, was well known for his religious work, most notably the tapestry "Christ in Glory" (1962) in the Coventry Cathedral. Recently, contemporary worship services are increasingly making use of visual media and works of arts. I know of a large congregation in California that regularly commissions works of art to mark the periods of the Christian year. Imagine the results if the leaders of our churches made a regular practice of encouraging, even commissioning, artists to prepare materials for the devotional and worship life of their churches. Or what if these artists were commissioned like missonaries to exercise their sanctified imaginations within the art world? Or in art schools?

Whether in the church or in the larger culture, we must learn to treasure the gifts of artistic imagination, for we are desperately in need of the "visions" of artists to help us prepare for that grand worship around the throne of God in heaven. In the end, just as the biblical story explodes in a dazzling display of images and songs, we long to see images of grace, to break out into song, or to dance before the Lord. For this to happen, we all need a deeper education in the visual arts, but even more we need a liberated imagination. Most of all we need a fresh filling of the Holy Spirit, who continues Christ's work of moving creatures to praise the Father.

A Restored Tradition of Christian Art

I dare to believe that one of the results of the Spirit coming upon God's people in fresh ways is that they will begin to imagine the shape of a restored tradition of Christian art. Or perhaps we should say a rekindling of the diverse Christian artistic heritage in our living worship life. We have spoken about the renewals that have taken place across the spectrum of Christian churches—the Catholic renewal since Vatican II, the Pentecostal and Charismatic renewal of the last century, the evangelical renewal since World War II—and the impact they have had on worship and the arts. Recently, there has been a new awakening both to the riches of older Christian art and its contemporary expression as well. One of the most successful recent exhibits in the National Gallery in London was on images of Christ, entitled "Seeing Salvation." Neil MacGregor, curator of the exhibit, presented a parallel series for the BBC and authored (with Erika Langmuir) a book to accompany the series, which explored the tradition of paintings of Christ.[3] This exhibit and book took up the question of how images of Christ can have meaning in a world without God, or how the suffering of this Christ could connect with a century that lived through Auschwitz. They also argued for the continued relevance of Christ's life and suffering. In Edmonton, Canada, David Goa brought together an important collection of historical and contemporary Christian art in a popular exhibit entitled "Anno Domini: Jesus through the Centuries," which uncovered the various styles in which Christians have given their witness to Christ.[4] Meanwhile, churches and denominations are developing resources for congregations to use that incorporate riches from many cultures and historical periods.[5]

In many respects, then, the pieces for forming a living tradition may already be visible around us, and they include contributions from many different art forms. Many have been touched by the spirituality, dance, and dramatics of black (and now thriving African and Latin American) churches. In the last generation, Christians have been blessed by a revival of serious music written out of deep Christian conviction by Arvo Part, John Tavaner, Henryk Górecki, Olivier Messiaen, and John Rutter. Such music has helped nourish our musical imagination. In the visual arts, there is a new visibility for Christian expression both in its medieval and contemporary forms. Christian arts groups and publications are appearing. Names of religious painters such as Stanley Spencer and Georges Rouault come up more frequently in discussions of twentieth-century art. Protestants have begun to appreciate and even reappropriate the best of our broader Christian heritage through the growing influence of the Catholic and Orthodox traditions. We have come to appreciate the visuality of the Ignatian tradition of prayers and the richness of icons in a devotional context. Since we share with these churches our deepest commitments to Christ and the power of the Spirit, why can't their worship practices become a part of the living heritage of our particular denomination?

But I need to express a caution at this point as well. In learning from the broader Christian tradition, we must take the time to recognize and appreciate the integrity of these traditions and the theological nuances they represent. Elements from various traditions cannot simply be spliced together in some makeshift fashion, as is too often the practice. They cannot be featured in a worship service as a kind of flavor of the month—this month we will use icons! Here is where careful historical and theological reflection must be a part of our reappropriation of the Christian tradition. We must consider critically what certain traditions represent, noting their weaknesses, even as we appreciate their contributions. As noted earlier, we must also be sensitive to the traditions and values of our own denominations and congregations. And we need careful and sensitive leaders who can guide us in the practices of worship in ways that honor the diversity of our heritage even as they develop new spiritual sensitivities.

But most importantly, we need the imaginative gifts of serious artists—those trained to blend harmonies, colors, even media in God-honoring ways. Great art will always be mediated through the consciousness of artists, whether they are working together or alone. It will not be conceived by committees or church leaders. Not that artists will work in an isolated ivory tower and come down with their inspired artworks. If our congregations embrace and love them and uphold them in prayer, these artists will be only too willing to collaborate with gifted members of the congregation in developing performances and spectacles that will reflect some of the splendor of Scripture, or even of God himself. We can thank God that these artists are present in our congregations in increasing numbers. But much work remains to be done in nurturing their talents. We must become better stewards of their gifts as we allow them to expand our corporate vision.

I have spoken of a possible Christian tradition of the arts. But in a way, this is a mistake, for we must speak not of a single tradition but of several, fed from one or another of the streams mentioned (and others not mentioned), each suited to its own cultural and historical context. It is important for each congregation, each denomination, to find styles and media with which they are comfortable— not trying promiscuously any style as though it were Saul's armor. We must ask God to allow us to bring out of our treasure house the talents that he has placed there and, as the Spirit inspires us, to make our unique image or to sing our particular melody of praise to God. And we need to press all the generations into service; we need the energy and visions of the youth, as well as the dreams of the older members. As H. R. Rookmaaker used to tell his students, "If you do your jobs, your grandchildren might make some modest contribution."

But the important thing is to imagine what might happen. Who has the courage to dream of performances of biblical audacity and scope? Of commissioned art to reflect the events of the Christian year? Or a collaboration of a visual artist with a musician for a special service? But for this transformation of our imagination we need the resources of the Spirit to provide a spiritual and theological depth that will sustain us for the long journey ahead. As Paul says (quoting Isaiah), "No eye has seen, nor ear heard, nor the human heart conceived, what God has prepared for those who love him. These things," Paul says, "God has revealed to us through the Spirit" (1 Cor. 2:9–10). For this renewal we work and pray.

notes

Preface

1. For this definition I owe a debt to Thomas Crow, *Modern Art in the Common Culture* (New Haven: Yale University Press, 1996), 211, and to Michael Rush, *New Media in Late Twentieth Century Art* (New York: Thames and Hudson, 1999), 7–9.

Introduction

1. Andrew Greeley, *The Catholic Imagination* (Berkeley: University of California, 2000), 42. Grace scale is discussed on pages 43–45.

2. Laurie Fendrich, "Why Abstract Painting Still Matters," *Chronicle of Higher Education,* 30 April 1999, B7.

3. Thomas McEvilley, "Two Big Shows: Post-Modernism and Its Discontent," *Artforum* (summer 1991): 99.

4. Fendrich, "Why Abstract Painting Still Matters," B5.

5. Thomas Crow, "On Mass Culture and Modernism," *Artforum* (summer 2000): 41–42.

6. See Herbert Gans, *Popular Culture and High Culture,* 2d ed. (New York: Free Press, 1999); and Paul Willis, *Common Culture: Symbolic Work at Play in the Everyday Cultures of the Young* (Boulder, Colo.: Westview Press, 1990). Nicholas Wolterstorff discusses the institution of high art in *Art in Action: Toward a Christian Aesthetic* (Grand Rapids: Eerdmans, 1980), chap. 1.

7. See Calvin Tompkins, *Post to Neo: The Art World of the 1980s* (New York: Penguin Books, 1988), 74. The number appears to be roughly the same ten years later. See the *New York Times,* Weekend, 5 May 2000, pp. B33, B36.

8. http://www.nytimes.com/2000/April/3/news/arts/museum-blockbusters.html.

9. Ibid.

10. An important voice in support of this point has been Thomas Crow. See *The Intelligence of Art* (Chapel Hill: University of North Carolina, 1999).

11. Willis, *Common Culture,* chap. 6. Cf. Thomas Crow: "Advanced art cannot live for long without the abandoned lower genres, and must now depend on the people into whose modest keeping those genres have fallen" (*Modern Art in the Common Culture,* 211).

12. Willis, *Common Culture,* 85.

13. See, for example, Jacques Ellul, *The Humiliation of the Word* (Grand Rapids: Eerdmans, 1985); and Neil Postman, *Amusing Ourselves to Death: Public Discourse in the Age of Show Business* (New York: Penguin Books, 1985).

14. I owe some of the thoughts in this paragraph to stimulating conversations with Dr. Willie Jennings of Duke University Divinity School.

15. See Wade Clark Roof, *A Generation of Seekers* (New York: HarperCollins, 1993).

16. Quoted in Makoto Fujimura, "River Grace," *Image: A Journal of the Arts and Religion* 22 (1999): 32.

17. Simone Weil, *Waiting on God,* ed. and trans. Emma Crawford (London: Routledge, Kegan and Paul, 1951), 101.

18. Quoted in Roberta Smith, "Spring Fireworks for the Old Art Hub," *New York Times,* 5 May 2000, p. B36.

19. In Ph.D. research for Fuller's School of World Mission, Chuck Fromm is currently finding that the Jesus People movement in the 1970s had a large impact not only on the musical world (in areas such as the development of Christian gospel) but also on the visual arts.

20. See John H. Wigger, *Taking Heaven by Storm: Methodism and the Rise of Popular Christianity in America* (New York: Oxford University Press, 1998).

21. Steve Scott, *Like a House on Fire: Renewal of the Arts in a Postmodern Culture* (Chicago: Cornerstone Press, 1997), 46.

Chapter 1

1. Paul C. Finney, *The Invisible God: The Earliest Christians on Art* (Oxford: Oxford University Press, 1994), 291.

2. Ibid., 293.

3. Dietrich Bonhoeffer, *Letters and Papers from Prison* (London: SCM, 1953).

4. Andre Grabar, *Christian Iconography: A Study of Its Origins* (Princeton: Princeton University Press, 1968), 15.

5. Thomas Mathews, *The Clash of the Gods: A Reinterpretation of Early Christian Art* (Princeton: Princeton University Press, 1993), 41, 43, 48. Mathews notes that there are at least twenty-eight sarcophagi depicting Christ's entry into Jerusalem. Many of the later images show Christ riding sidesaddle.

6. Ibid., 180.

7. Grabar, *Christian Iconography,* 9.

8. Margaret Miles, *Image as Insight* (Boston: Beacon Press, 1985), chap. 1.

9. Mathews, *Clash of the Gods,* 11.

10. Bede, *Ecclesiastical History,* I, xxx, ed. Bertram Colgrave and R. A. B. Mynors (Oxford: Clarendon Press, 1969), 107.

11. St. Augustine, *On Christian Doctrine,* trans. D. W. Robertson Jr. (New York: Library of Liberal Arts, 1958), 10.

12. Ibid., 15.

13. Peter Brown, *The Cult of the Saints* (Chicago: University of Chicago Press, 1981), 53.

14. Ibid., 98–99.

15. "Dionysius, the Pseudo-Areopagite," in *The Oxford Dictionary of the Christian Church,* 2d ed., ed. F. L. Cross (Oxford: Oxford University Press, 1974), 406.

16. Bernard McGinn, John Meyendorff, and Jean Leclerq, eds., *Christian Spirituality: Origins to the Twelfth Century* (New York: Crossroad, 1987), 134.

17. Gervase Mathew, *Byzantine Aesthetics* (New York: Harper & Row, 1971), 94–107.

18. This is described and discussed in Sister Charles Murray's important article, "Art in the Early Church," *Journal of Theological Studies* 28 (1977): 343–44.

19. Mathew points out that for Byzantine art this had an important theological meaning. It asserted the full humanity of Christ, which supporters of icons felt the iconoclasts were implicitly denying. "Byzantine art would always be concerned principally with the human figure" (*Byzantine Aesthetics,* 56). Interestingly, the human body later became the central symbol of the Renaissance, perhaps through the Byzantine influence on that period of art. See Deno John Geanakopolos, *Constantine and the East: Essays on the Late Byzantine and Italian Renaissance and the Byzantine and Roman Churches* (Madison: University of Wisconsin, 1989).

20. Quoted in Thomas F. Mathews, *Byzantium: From Antiquity to the Renaissance* (New York: Abrams, 1998), 56.

21. John of Damascus, *On the Divine Images, First Apology,* 8, trans. David Anderson (Crestwood, N.Y.: St. Vladimir's Press, 1980), 18.

22. Ibid.

23. The church as a symbol of Noah's ark, which saved the righteous from the waters of destruction, was an idea first introduced by Cyprian in the third century and became a common notion during the Middle Ages.

24. Actually, communion in both kinds was rare in the medieval period; usually laypeople took only the wafer.

25. An excellent survey of the Gothic tradition is found in Emile Mâle, *The Gothic Image: Religious Art in the Thirteenth Century* (London: Collins, 1961).

26. Erich Auerbach, *Mimesis: The Representation of Reality in Western Literature* (Princeton: Princeton University Press, 1953), 148.

27. John Dixon Jr., "Painting as Theological Thought: Issues in Tuscan Theology," in *Creativity and the Sacred,* ed. Diane Apostolos-Cappadona (New York: Rinehart and Winston, 1984), 289.

28. Ibid., 285.

29. Ibid., 281.

30. *Italian Panel Painting of the Early Renaissance* (Los Angeles: Los Angeles County Museum of Art, 1995).

31. Dante Alighieri, *Paradiso,* trans. John Ciardi (New York: Norton, 1961), canto XXXIII, lines 98, 99, and 137, 138.

32. Timothy Verdon, "Christianity, the Renaissance, and the Study of History: Environments of Experience and Imagination," in *Christianity and the Renaissance: Image and Religious Imagination in the Quattrocento,* ed. Timothy Verdon and John Henderson (Syracuse: Syracuse University Press, 1990), 12.

33. This movement "gave impetus to the visual arts . . . owing to the support of the wealthy lay patrons attracted by the reformers' energy and obvious sincerity" (ibid., 22).

34. Dugald McLellan, *Singorelli's Orvieto Frescoes: A Guide to the Cappella Nuova* (Orvieto: Quattroemme, 1998), 22.

35. Quoted in Margaret Miles, "The Revelatory Body: Signorelli's 'Resurrection of the Flesh' at Orvieto," *Theological Education* 21, no. 1 (1994): 80.

36. The full title is *The Sexuality of Christ in Renaissance Art and in Modern Oblivion,* 2d ed. (New York: A Pantheon/October Book, 1983, 1996).

Chapter 2

1. Thomas à Kempis, *The Imitation of Christ,* trans. Abbot Justin McCann (New York: Mentor/New American Library, 1957), 142.

2. John Walford of Wheaton College is currently doing important research in this area that supports this hypothesis. I am indebted to him for conversations that illumined this period.

3. John Calvin, *Institutes of the Christian Religion,* ed. John McNeill, trans. Ford Lewis Battles (Philadelpia: Westminster Press, 1960), I, xi, 5.

4. Ibid., I, xi, 7.

5. Ibid.

6. Ibid., I, xi, 12.

7. Ibid., I, xiv, 20.

8. Ibid., I, x, 1.

9. See, for example, the chapter entitled "Paul and the Introspective Conscience of the West," in Krister Stendahl, *Paul among Jews and Gentiles* (Minneapolis: Fortress Press, 1976).

10. John Drury, *Painting the Word: Christian Pictures and Their Meanings* (New Haven: Yale University Press, 1999), 32. Drury also speaks of the change from objective to subjective piety. I prefer "personal" to avoid the modern connotations associated with "subjective."

11. Miles, *Image as Insight,* 17.

12. Charles Garside, *Zwingli and the Arts* (New Haven: Yale University Press, 1966), 175.

13. E. John Walford, *Jacob van Ruisdael and the Perception of Landscape* (New Haven: Yale University Press, 1991), esp. 138–40.

14. Originally this was proposed by Abraham Kuyper in his Stone Lectures, in the chapter "Calvinsim and the Arts," and was reiterated by H. R. Rookmaaker, *Modern Art and the Death of a Culture* (Downers Grove, Ill.: InterVarsity Press, 1971). But it has recently been questioned by Reindert L. Falkenburg, "Calvinism and the Emergence of a Seventeenth-Century Dutch Landscape Art—A Critical Evaluation," in *Seeing beyond the Word: Visual Arts and the Calvinist Tradition,* ed. Paul Corby Finney (Grand Rapids: Eerdmans, 1999), 343–68.

15. See Philip Benedict, "Calvinism as a Culture?" in *Seeing beyond the Word: Visual Arts and the Calvinist Tradition,* ed. Paul Corby Finney (Grand Rapids: Eerdmans, 1999), 36 n. 54.

16. The first formulation of this hierarchy was André Félibien, Conférences de l'Académie royale de peinture et de sculpture, Paris, 1668, and is discussed in the modern context by Crow, *Modern Art in the Common Culture,* chap. 10. Félibien did not, of course, include the genre that later came to be called "pastoral." This was not then felt to be edifying.

17. Jonathan Edwards, *Religious Affections* (Carlisle, Pa: Banner of Truth Trust, 1961), 213–14. Beauty for Edwards is related to the moral excellency of God, which also shines in creation. Cf. 179, 182.

18. I have developed this idea in more detail in *How Does America Hear the Gospel?* (Grand Rapids: Eerdmans, 1989), chap. 3.

19. See Roger Lundin, "Offspring of an Odd Union: Evangelical Attitudes toward the Arts," in *Evangelicalism and Modern America,* ed. George Marsden (Grand Rapids: Eerdmans, 1984), 138–40. Their attitude toward the past reflected the view that "cultural discontinuity [is] a liberating force which allows the artist to act like God" (140).

20. Robert Crawford, "Presbyterianism and Imagination in Modern Scotland," in *Scotland's Shame: Bigotry and Sectarianism in Modern Scotland,* ed. T. M. Devine (Edinburgh: Mainstream Publishing, 2000), 189.

21. Robert Hughes, *Shock of the New: The Life and Death of Modern Art* (New York: Knopf, 1981).

22. This kind of art has typically been overlooked by scholars, but this situation has recently begun to change. See David Morgan's excellent book, *Visual Piety* (Berkeley: University of California, 1998), and also his *Protestant and Pictures* (Oxford: Oxford University Press, 2000).

23. For Tillich's writings on art, see John and Jane Dillenberger, eds., *Paul Tillich: Writings on Art and Architecture* (New York: Crossroad, 1987). Reference to the war is found on page 126. A helpful discussion of Tillich is Jeremy Begbie, *Voicing Creation's Praise* (Edinburgh: Blackwell, 1991), 1–77.

24. Dillenberger, *Paul Tillich,* 129.

25. Ibid., 133 n. 3.

26. Ibid., 173.

27. Ibid., 141.

28. See discussion in Begbie, *Voicing Creation's Praise,* 68–74.

29. Ibid., 182.

30. Francis Schaeffer's books dealt more generally with apologetic presentation of Christian truth (see *The God Who Is There* [Downers Grove, Ill.: InterVarsity Press, 1968]), but he wrote a small book called *Art and the Bible* (Downers Grove, Ill.: InterVarsity Press, 1973). Rookmaaker's best-known book is *Modern Art and the Death of a Culture.* A complete edition of Rookmaaker's works is in preparation (Carlisle: Piquant, forthcoming). See the survey in Begbie, *Voicing Creation's Praise,* 81–163.

31. Rookmaaker, *Modern Art and the Death of a Culture,* 228. See, for example, Wolterstorff, *Art in Action;* and Calvin Seerveld, *Rainbows for the Fallen World: Aesthetic Life and Artistic Task* (Toronto: Tuppence Press, 1980).

32. See my study of Rouault, where the revival is also described in some detail: *Rouault: A Vision of Suffering and Salvation* (Grand Rapids: Eerdmans, 1971).

33. Though there are no doubt other factors as well. One thinks, for example, of the increasing contact with nonwestern cultures and the growing visibility of so-called minority cultures in America (and elsewhere in the West).

34. Cynthia Pearl Maus, *Christ and the Fine Arts* (New York: Harper Brothers, 1938), extending to 764 pages!

35. See Finley Eversole, ed., *Christian Faith and the Contemporary Arts* (New York: Abingdon Press, 1957); and Nathan A. Scott Jr., *The New Orpheus: Essays toward a Christian Poetic* (New York: Sheed and Ward, 1964).

36. See Roger Hazelton, *A Theological Approach to Art* (New York: Abingdon Press, 1967); and Donald Whittle, *Christianity and the Arts* (Philadelphia: Fortress Press, 1966).

37. G. Wilson Knight, *The Christian Renaissance* (London: Methuen and Co., 1962).

38. See Gerhardus Van der Leeuw, *Sacred and Profane Beauty* (New York: Holt, Rinehart and Winston, 1963).

39. Derek Kidner, *The Christian and the Arts* (Chicago: InterVarsity Press, 1959); Calvin Seerveld, *A Christian Critique of Art and Literature* (Toronto: Association for Reformed Scientific Studies, 1968); and D. Bruce Lockerbie, *The Liberating Word: Art and the Mystery of the Gospel* (Grand Rapids: Eerdmans, 1974).

40. See the special issue of the journal *Theological Education* called "Sacred Imagination: The Arts and Theological Education," ed. Wilson Yates, 31, no. 1 (autumn 1994).

Chapter 3

1. C. S. Lewis, "Christianity and Culture," in *Christian Reflections,* ed. Walter Hooper (Grand Rapids: Eerdmans, 1967), 12–36. Lewis here reflects a point of view that reaches back through John Henry Newman to the medieval distinction (even separation) between nature and grace, which I noted in Thomas Aquinas and Dante.

2. Kidner, *The Christian and the Arts,* 5. In fairness, Kidner himself goes on to show that this is not the end of the story, making a strong biblical case for good art.

3. I am summarizing here a longer study on biblical language for beauty: W. A. Dyrness, "Aesthetics in the Old Testament: Beauty in Context," *Journal of the Evangelical Theological Society* 28, no. 4 (December 1985): 421–32.

4. These word groups, while central to Old Testament descriptions of beauty as we understand it, do not comprise the totality of what we might study. Words for "goodness" (*tob*) or "glory" (*kabod*) might also well be examined for their aesthetic implications. But I leave these for special comment below.

5. Aware of the dangers of isolated word studies, I employ here the methodology used by H. W. Wolff in *Anthropology of the Old Testament* (Philadelphia: Fortress Press, 1974), 3–9, where he uses a variety of words to develop a semantic field.

6. Interestingly, in Hebrew there is no equivalent for the word *ugly*. The closest is *blemish* or *defect (mum* and *me'umah),* which can be either physical or moral and can disqualify one from priestly service. In a sense, "ugly" is any defect that keeps something from being what it is created to be.

7. Calvin Seerveld, "The Relation of the Arts to the Presentation of the Truth," in *Truth and Reality: Philosophical Perspectives on Reality,* ed. Hendrik Gerhardus (Braamfotein, S.A.: DeJohng's Bookshop, 1971), 162.

8. Walter Brueggemann, *The Prophetic Imagination* (Philadelphia: Fortress Press, 1978), 49. Cf. 77ff. on prophetic images of hope.

9. Othmer Keel, *Symbolism of the Biblical World: Ancient Near Eastern Iconography and the Book of Psalms* (New York: Seabury Press, 1978), 20. Cf. A. N. Wilder: "We underestimate the grace of God if we do not recognize that it blesses us not only with his presence and call, but also with illumination of the ways of the world and his ways with it" (*Theopoetic: Theology and the Religious Imagination* [Philadelphia: Fortress Press, 1967], 92). John Calvin understood this pedagogical purpose of images, as God takes us by the hand, leading us by the Old Testament ceremonies to the mediator. Cf. L. Wencelius, *L'esthétique de Calvin* (1937; reprint, Geneva: Slatkire Reprints, 1979), 194.

10. Keel, *Symbolism of the Biblical World.* Keel describes these images with the German word *Denkbild* ("thought picture").

11. Ibid., 77ff.

12. See Hans Urs von Balthasar, *La gloire et la croix: Les aspect esthétiques de la révélation,* vol. 1 (Aubier: Ed Montigne, 1965), 17.

13. Eric Werner, *The Sacred Bridge* (New York: Columbia, 1958), 313.

14. Cf. Thorlief Boman, *Hebrew Thought Compared with Greek* (Philadelphia: Westminster, 1960), 83.

15. Claus Westermann, "Biblische Ästhetik," *Die Zeichen der Zeit* 4 (1950): 280–81.

16. G. von Rad, *Wisdom in Israel* (London: SCM, 1972), 25.

17. See William A. Dyrness, "The 'Imago Dei' and Biblical Aesthetics," *Journal of the Evangelical Theological Society* (summer 1974): 161–72.

18. von Balthasar, *La gloire et la croix,* 279–85.

19. 1937, now in Madrid. This work has been called a "devastating attack on man's cruelty and folly" (David Piper, ed., *The Random House Dictionary of Art and Artists* [New York: Random House, 1981], 405).

Chapter 4

1. Quoted by David Deitcher in "Barbara Kruger: Resisting Arrest," *Artforum* 29, no. 6 (February 1991): 84.

2. Quoted in Jean Leclerq, "Prayer in the West," in *Christian Spirituality: Origins to the Twelfth Century,* ed. Bernard McGinn, John Meyendorff, and Jean Leclerq (New York: Crossroad, 1987), 395.

3. Quoted in Gervase Mathew, *Byzantine Aesthetics,* 105.

4. Ibid., 107.

5. Greeley, *Catholic Imagination,* passim.

6. Jacques Maritain, *Creative Intuition in Art and Poetry* (Cleveland: Meridian; New York: World Publishing, 1954).

7. Ibid., 39.

8. Ibid., 84.

9. Ibid., 100.

10. Ibid., 57.

11. Ibid., 292.

12. Patrick Sherry, *Spirit and Beauty: An Introduction to Theological Aesthetics* (Oxford: Clarendon, 1992), 2.

13. Ibid., 113.

14. Ibid., 154. A similar point is made in John Navone, *Toward a Theology of Beauty* (Collegeville, Minn.: Liturgical Press, 1996), 24: "True beauty as attractiveness of the truly good motivates human development in that intellectual, moral and religious self-transcendence that constitutes human authenticity."

15. von Balthasar, *La gloire et la croix,* 17.

16. Ibid., 26.

17. Ibid., 29.

18. Ibid., 104.

19. Interestingly, von Balthasar himself says, "A character of enthusiasm, in the theological sense of the word, impregnates the whole of revelation" (ibid., 102).

20. Wolterstorff, *Art in Action,* 70.

21. Jürgen Moltmann, *The Coming of God: Christian Eschatology,* ed. Margaret Kohl (Minneapolis: Fortress Press, 1996), 334.

22. Ibid., 336.

23. Colin Gunton, *The Triune Creator* (Grand Rapids: Eerdmans, 1998), 143. The context is the larger discussion of the mediation of Christ in creation, as the means by which God goes out into that which is not God.

24. Jeremy Begbie, *Voicing Creation's Praise: Towards a Theology of the Arts* (Edinburgh: Blackwell, 1991), 170, 174.

25. Ibid., 179.

26. Jeremy Begbie, *Theology, Music, and Time* (Cambridge: Cambridge University Press, 2000), 80.

27. Ibid., 239.

28. Trevor Hart, "Hearing, Seeing, and Touching the Truth," in *Beholding the Glory: Incarnation through the Arts,* ed. Jeremy Begbie (Grand Rapids: Baker, 2000), 1–25.

29. Ibid., 25.

30. Begbie, *Voicing Creation's Praise,* 228.

31. Ibid., 173.

32. I have reviewed some of this discussion in my *Earth Is God's: A Theology of American Culture* (Maryknoll, N.Y.: Orbis, 1997), chap. 3.

33. Rookmaaker, *Modern Art and the Death of a Culture,* 36.

34. Ibid., 211.

35. Ibid., 220ff.

36. Ibid., 225.

37. Ibid., 228.

38. Ibid., 243.

39. Ibid., 228.

40. Though we stop short of saying that artists are prophets in the sense often used in modern art. This view, which has its roots in the Romantic view of the artist, often exaggerates the extent that artists can see and capture the essence of reality. See H. R. Rookmaaker's self-published booklet "Artist as Prophet" (Amsterdam, 1968).

41. Wolterstorff, *Art in Action,* 70.

42. Ibid., 49.

43. Ibid., 71.

44. Ibid., 92.

45. Ibid., 95.

46. Begbie, *Voicing Creation's Praise,* 145–48.

47. Wolterstorff, *Art in Action,* 67–69.

48. I have developed this further in *The Earth Is God's,* 142–47.

49. In this sense, art that is valid and good does not necessarily praise the Creator; in some cases, it may better be described as a curse.

50. I have elaborated on these themes in chapter 6 of *The Earth Is God's.* We will explore the nature of this rest in chapter 6.

51. "Allusive" is from Calvin Seerveld and underlines the suggestive, symbolic character of art. See Seerveld, *Rainbows for the Fallen World.*

52. George Steiner has argued eloquently that all art rests on and responds to the presence of the Logos in reality, though he does not give this the trinitarian shape that Christians do. See his *Real Presences: Is There Anything in What We Say?* (London: Faber and Faber, 1989).

53. Nicholas Cook, *Music: A Very Short Introduction* (Oxford: Oxford University Press, 1998), 78.

54. Ibid., 85.

Chapter 5

1. Crow, *Modern Art in the Common Culture,* 211.

2. Rensselaer W. Lee, "Ut Pictura Poesis: The Humanistic Theory of Painting," *Art Bulletin* 22 (1940): 201.

3. Janine Bailly-Herberg, ed., *Correspondence de Camille Pissarro,* vol. 1 (Paris: Presse Universitaire de France, 1980), 253. The term he uses suggests that one actually creates a "double" of oneself.

4. See William Seitz's discussion in *Claude Monet 1840–1926* (New York: Abrams, 1960).

5. Gerard Manley Hopkins, "Pied Beauty," in *The New Oxford Book of English Verse,* ed. Helen Gardner (Oxford: Oxford University Press, 1972), 787.

6. Ibid., "God's Grandeur," 724.

7. G. K. Chesterton quoted in Colin Gunton, *The One, The Three, and the Many* (Cambridge: Cambridge University Press, 1993), 192–93.

8. Robert Pippin quoted in ibid.

9. Rush, *New Media in Late Twentieth Century Art,* 21.

10. These points are made in Crow, *Modern Art in the Common Culture,* 24–25.

11. Quoted in J. H. Mathews, *An Introduction to Surrealism* (College Station, Pa.: Penn State University Press, 1965), 43ff.

12. Ibid., 60.

13. Pollock, for his part, was irritated by the way his intense efforts and discipline were dismissed. See Crow, *Modern Art in the Common Culture,* chap. 2, esp. 42.

14. Clive Bell, *Art* (New York: Frederick Stokes, 1913), 27.

15. Clement Greenberg, *Art and Culture: Critical Essays* (Boston: Beacon Press, 1961), 136.

16. Greenberg wrote, "Pollock has a superlative instinct for resounding appositions of light and dark, and at the same time he is lone in his power to assert a point strewn or paint laden surface as a single synoptic vision" (ibid., 217).

17. Quoted in Rush, *New Media in Late Twentieth Century Art,* 36.

18. A Christian expression of this point of view that has been influential is represented by Dorothy Sayers. See *The Mind of the Maker* (London: Methuen, 1941).

19. I am indebted to the discussion of this in Nicholas Cook, *Music, Imagination, and Culture* (Oxford: Oxford University Press, 1990), 181–82.

20. Wassily Kandinsky, *Concerning the Spiritual in Art* (New York: Dover Books, 1977). See 6ff. for the description of the triangle.

21. Ibid., 20.

22. Robert Hughes, "Decline and Fall of the Avant-Garde," *Time,* 18 December 1972, 111–12.

23. Ibid.

24. Ibid.

25. James S. Ackerman, "The Demise of the Avant Garde: Notes on the Sociology of Recent American Art," *Comparative Studies in Society and History* 11 (1969): 371–84.

26. Ibid., 379.

27. This term was first used by Charles Jenks about architecture but subsequently was applied to other visual arts. See Charles Jenks, *The Language of Post-Modern Architecture,* 4th ed. (London: Academy Editions, 1984). These movements are chronicled in Steven Connor, *Post-Modernist Culture: An Introduction to Theories of the Contemporary* (Oxford: Blackwell, 1989).

28. Quoted in Dominic Aquila, "The Music of Arvo Part," *Image: A Journal of the Arts and Religion* (summer 1992): 116. Note again the iconoclastic overtones.

29. Quoted in Crow, *Modern Art in Common Culture,* 77.

30. Diane Apostolos-Cappadona, ed., *Art, Creativity, and the Sacred* (New York: Crossroad, 1986), 21.

31. Suzi Gablik, *Has Modernism Failed?* (New York: Thames and Hudson, 1984), 76.

32. Suzi Gablik, "Reclaiming a Sacred Vision," *Art Papers* 10, no. 6 (November/December 1986): 4.

33. See Suzi Gablik, *The Re-enchantment of Art* (New York: Thames and Hudson, 1991).

Chapter 6

1. Quoted in Rush, *New Media in Late Twentieth Century Art,* 8.

2. Christopher Knight, "Thematically Overwrought," *Los Angeles Times,* 23 October 2000, pp. F1, F11.

3. Robert Smith, "Memo to Art Museums: Don't Give Up on Art," *New York Times,* 3 December 2000, sect. 2, pp. 1, 35.

4. Lynn Aldrich, "Through Sculpture: What's the Matter with Matter?" in *Beholding the Glory,* 109.

5. Quoted in William Dyrness, "Whispers in Ordinary Time: The Art of Lynn Aldrich," *Image: A Journal of the Arts and Religion* 19 (spring 1998): 61.

6. Ibid.

7. Cook, *Music,* 78.

8. Jonathan Jones, "Shock Treatment," *The Guardian* (7 September 2000): 2–3.

9. Willis, *Common Culture,* 49. He also notes how advertising itself has to become collaborative with film, sports, and music to be effective.

10. Ibid., 10, 59.

11. Tompkins, *Post to Neo,* 96.

12. See Ellul, *Humiliation of the Word.*

13. Ibid., 5–8.

14. See Ellul's landmark study *The Technological Society* (New York: Knopf, 1964).

15. Ibid., 12.

16. Ibid., 3, 14.

17. Ibid., 80.

18. Ibid., 83.

19. Postman, *Amusing Ourselves to Death,* 18.

20. Ibid., 28.

21. Ibid., 29.

22. See Jacques Barzun, *From Dawn to Decadence: Five Hundred Years of Western Cultural Life, 1500–2000* (New York: HarperCollins, 2000).

23. See Gans, *Popular Culture and High Culture.*

24. Mitchell Stephens, *The Rise of the Image and the Fall of the Word* (Oxford: Oxford University Press, 1998), xi.

25. Ibid., 11.

26. Ibid., 105.

27. Ibid., 153.

28. Ibid., 170.

29. Ibid., 183.

30. Ibid., 189–90.

31. Ibid., 197.

32. Ibid., 208.

33. Ibid., 215.

34. Alex Grey, "The Artist as Visionary," *Los Angeles Times,* 8 May 1999, p. F6.

35. Christopher Knight, "LeWitt Turns the Logical into the Spiritual," *Los Angeles Times,* 8 March 2000, p. F14.

36. Gablik, "Reclaiming a Sacred Vision," 4.

37. Robin Sylvan, "Traces of the Spirit: The Religious Dimension of Popular Music" (Ph.D. diss., University of California at Santa Barbara, 1998).

38. Gerald Marzorati, "Julian Schnabel: Plate It as It Lays" *Art News* 85, no. 4 (April 1985): 69.

39. Peter Fuller, *Images of God: The Consolations of Lost Illusions* (London: Hogarth Press, 1990), 311.

40. William Blake, "Jerusalem," in *The Complete Poetry of John Donne and William Blake* (New York: Random House, 1941), 1016.

41. Quoted by Fujimura, "River Grace," 33.

42. Ibid., 35.

43. Ibid., 40.

44. In Verdon and Henderson, eds., *Christianity and the Renaissance,* 378.

45. See Fiona Bond, *The Arts in Your Church* (Carlisle: Piquant, 2001), for helpful suggestions as to how you can implement these ideas in your church.

46. I am grateful to Chuck Fromm for pointing this out in a class lecture, 11 May 2000, at Fuller Seminary.

Chapter 7

1. In 2000, Karen Mulder conducted an informal survey of art departments in Christian schools and found that the top fourteen departments sent no more than one or two graduates each year to graduate school in the fine arts. These twenty-five students who go on for their MFA, while certainly representing an increase over a generation ago, are certainly too few in number to make much of an impact on the art world. Personal communication, 9 February 2001.

2. Some of this may have to do with a general suspicion of "institutions" that characterizes the generations sometimes called the Xers and the Millennial generation. Many in these groups are open to spirituality but turned off by religion.

3. There are deep historical and cultural factors as to why this debilitating dichotomy exists. Two good books that address these issues are Eric Gill, *The Holy Tradition of Working* (Ipswich: Gogonooza Press, 1983); and Robert K. Johnston, *The Christian at Play* (Grand Rapids: Eerdmans, 1983).

4. T. S. Eliot, "Literary Criticism," in Helen Louise Gardner, *Religion and Literature: Selected Essays* (London: Faber and Faber, 1934), 395–98 (quote is from page 398).

5. Elaine Scarry, *On Beauty and Being Just* (Princeton: Princeton University Press, 1999), 25–26. Scarry's beautiful book is an illustration of the apologetic problem that nonbelievers have set for themselves. If Christians have to account for the presence of evil in the world, nonbelievers have an opposite problem, what might be called the problem of the good. If the Christian must ask, "How can evil invade such a good world?" the nonbeliever must ask, "If the world has no purpose, whence goodness or beauty?" Scarry's book addresses this question.

6. Ibid., 47–48.

7. Though it is an argument that Steiner makes in *Real Presences.*

8. Augustine, *Confessions,* IV, 7, 10, trans. R. S. Pine-Coffin (Harmondsworth: Penguin, 1961), 78, 80.

9. Crow, *Modern Art in the Common Culture,* 33.

10. C. S. Lewis, *An Experiment in Criticism* (Cambridge: Cambridge University Press, 1961), 137, 140 (quote is from page 140).

11. Navone, *Theology of Beauty,* 24.

12. The term "redemptive wish" is from Thomas Crow. In speaking of the work of Christopher Williams, Crow notes how his photographs are leavened with signs of hope and beauty. "The glass flowers exert their power by standing as tokens for this redemptive wish—as art has often done" (*Modern Art in the Common Culture,* 200).

13. What follows in the rest of this section is adapted from "The World of Art Is a Dirty Place . . . What Becomes of Christian Purity?" Christians in the Visual Arts Newsletter 8, no. 1 (March 2000): 8. Used by permission.

14. Scarry, *On Beauty and Being Just,* 110.

15. Ibid., 111.

16. Ibid.

17. Simone Weil, *Waiting for God,* trans. Emma Craufurd (New York: Harper & Row, 1951), 158–59, from which Scarry also quotes.

18. Ibid.

19. Madeleine L'Engle, *Walking on Water: Reflections on Faith and Art* (Wheaton: Harold Shaw Publishers, 1980), 189.

20. T. S. Eliot, "Burnt Norton V," *The Complete Poems and Plays of T. S. Eliot* (New York: Harcourt Brace and Co., 1952), 121.

21. Wolterstorff, *Art in Action,* 95.

22. Letter from Arles, April 1888, in Herschel B. Chipp, *Theories of Modern Art: A Sourcebook by Artists and Critics* (Berkeley: University of California, 1970), 32.

23. L'Engle, *Walking on Water,* 195.

Conclusion

1. James Torrance, *Worship, Community, and the Triune God of Grace* (Downers Grove, Ill.: InterVarsity Press, 1996), 30.

2. Hughes Oliphant Olds, *Themes and Variations for a Christian Doxology: Some Thoughts on the Theology of Worship* (Grand Rapids: Eerdmans, 1992), 8. He goes on to quote Ephesians 1:12, where Paul notes that in Christ we "have been destined and appointed to live to the praise of [God's] glory."

3. Neil MacGregor with Erika Langmuir, *Seeing Salvation: Images of Christ in Art* (New Haven: Yale University Press, 2000). John Drury earlier published a widely acclaimed study of Christian paintings at the National Gallery: *Painting the Word: Christian Pictures and Their Meanings* (New Haven: Yale University Press, 1999).

4. See the catalog by David Goa, *Anno Domini: Jesus through the Centuries* (Edmonton: Provincial Museum of Alberta, 2000).

5. See, for example, Susan A. Blain, ed., *Imaging the Word: An Arts and Lectionary Resource,* vol. 3 (Cleveland: United Church Press, 1996); and Bond, *Arts in Your Church.*

bibliography

Books

Apostolos-Cappadona, Diane, ed. *Art, Creativity, and the Sacred.* New York: Cross-road, 1986.

Auerbach, E. *Mimesis: The Representation of Reality in Western Literature.* Princeton: Princeton University Press, 1953.

Begbie, Jeremy. *Theology, Music, and Time.* Cambridge: Cambridge University Press, 2000.

—————. *Voicing Creation's Praise: Towards a Theology of the Arts.* Edinburgh: Black-well, 1991.

—————, ed. *Beholding the Glory: Incarnation through the Arts.* Grand Rapids: Baker, 2000.

Blain, Susan A., ed. *Imaging the Word: An Arts and Lectionary Resource.* Vol. 3. Cleve-land: United Church Press, 1996.

Bond, Fiona. *The Arts in Your Church.* Carlisle: Piquant, 2001.

Brand, Hilary, and Adrienne Chaplin. *Art and Soul: Signposts for Christians in the Arts.* Carlisle: Solway, 1999.

Brown, Frank Burch. *Religious Aesthetics: A Theological Study of Making and Mean-ing.* Princeton: Princeton University Press, 1989.

Couturier, M. Z. *Sacred Art.* Austin: University of Texas Press, 1983.

Crow, Thomas. *Modern Art in the Common Culture.* New Haven: Yale University Press, 1996.

Dillenberger, Jane. *Style and Content in Christian Art.* New York: Crossroad, 1988.

Dillenberger, John. *Images and Relics: Theological Perceptions and Visual Images in Sixteenth Century Europe*. Oxford: Oxford University Press, 1999.

———. *A Theology of Artistic Sensitivities*. New York: Crossroad, 1986.

Drury, John. *Painting the Word: Christian Pictures and Their Meanings*. New Haven: Yale University Press, 1999.

Dyrness, William. *Christian Art in Asia*. Amsterdam: Rodopi, 1979.

———. *The Earth Is God's: A Theology of American Culture*. Maryknoll, N.Y.: Orbis, 1997.

———. *Rouault: A Vision of Suffering and Salvation*. Grand Rapids: Eerdmans, 1971.

Eco, Umberto. *Art and Beauty in the Middle Ages*. New Haven: Yale University Press, 1986.

Evdokimov, Paul. *The Art of the Icon: A Theology of Beauty*. Translated by Steven Bigham. Redondo Beach, Calif.: Oakwood Publications, 1990.

Finney, Paul Corby, ed. *Seeing beyond the Word: Visual Arts and the Calvinist Tradition*. Grand Rapids: Eerdmans, 1999.

Fuller, Peter. *Images of God: The Consolations of Lost Illusions*. London: Hogarth Press, 1990.

Gablik, Suzi. *Has Modernism Failed?* New York: Thames and Hudson, 1984.

———. *The Re-enchantment of Art*. New York: Thames and Hudson, 1991.

Greeley, Andrew. *The Catholic Imagination*. Berkeley: University of California, 2000.

Hofstadter, Albert, and Richard Kuhns, eds. *Philosophies of Art and Beauty: Selected Readings in Aesthetics from Plato to Heidegger*. Chicago: University of Chicago, 1976.

Hughes, Robert. *Shock of the New: The Life and Death of Modern Art*. New York: Knopf, 1981.

Kuyper, Abraham. *Lectures on Calvinism*. Grand Rapids: Eerdmans, 1931.

MacGregor, Neil, with Erika Langmuir. *Seeing Salvation: Images of Christ in Art*. New Haven: Yale, 2000.

Maritain, Jacques. *Art and Scholasticism and the Frontiers of Poetry*. New York: Scribners, 1962.

———. *Creative Intuition in Art and Poetry*. Cleveland: Meridian; New York: World Publishing, 1954.

Miles, Margaret R. *Image as Insight: Visual Understanding in Western Christianity and Secular Culture*. Boston: Beacon Press, 1985.

Morgan, David. *Visual Piety*. Berkeley: University of California, 1998.

Navone, John. *Toward a Theology of Beauty*. Collegeville, Minn.: Liturgical Press, 1996.

Pattison, George. *Art, Modernity, and Faith*. New York: St. Martin's Press, 1991.

Rookmaaker, H. R. *The Creative Gift: Essays on Art and the Christian Life*. Westchester, Ill.: Cornerstone Books, 1981.

———. *Modern Art and the Death of a Culture*. Downers Grove, Ill.: InterVarsity Press, 1971.

Rush, Michael. *New Media in Late Twentieth Century Art.* London: Thames and Hudson, 1999.

Scarry, Elaine. *On Beauty and Being Just.* Princeton: Princeton University Press, 1999.

Schaeffer, Francis. *Art and the Bible.* Downers Grove, Ill.: InterVarsity Press, 1973.

———. *The God Who Is There.* Downers Grove, Ill.: InterVarsity Press, 1968.

Seerveld, Calvin. *Rainbows for the Fallen World: Aesthetic Life and Artistic Task.* Toronto: Tuppence Press, 1980.

Steiner, George. *Real Presences: Is There Anything in What We Say?* London: Faber and Faber, 1989.

Stevens, Mitchell. *The Rise of the Image and the Fall of the Word.* Oxford: Oxford University Press, 1998.

Takenaka, Masao. *Christian Art in Asia.* Tokyo: Kyo Bun Kwan, 1975.

Tillich, Paul. *Theology of Culture.* New York: Oxford University Press, 1959.

Tolstoy, Leo. *What Is Art?* Edited by Alymer Maude. Indianapolis: Bobbs-Merrill, 1960.

Veith, Gene E., Jr. *State of the Arts: From Bezalel to Mapplethorpe.* Westchester, Ill.: Crossway Books, 1991.

Viladesau, Richard. *Theology and the Arts: Encountering God through Music, Art, and Rhetoric.* New York: Paulist Press, 2000.

Walford, John. *Jacob van Ruisdael and the Perception of Landscape.* New Haven: Yale University Press, 1991.

Willis, Paul. *Common Culture: Symbolic Work at Play in the Everyday Cultures of the Young.* Boulder, Colo.: Westview Press, 1990.

Wolterstorff, Nicholas. *Art in Action: Toward a Christian Aesthetic.* Grand Rapids: Eerdmans, 1980.

Journals

Arts: The Arts in Religious and Theological Studies, 300 Fifth Street NW, New Brighton, MN 55112

Christianity and the Arts, P.O. Box 118088, Chicago, IL 60611

Image: A Journal of the Arts and Religion, P.O. Box 3000, Denville, NJ 07834

Organizations

Artists in Christian Testimony, ACT, Box 395, Franklin, TN 37065-0395 (a mission organization devoted to mobilizing and equipping Christian arts and music communicators for ministry; Byron Spradlin, director).

Christians in the Visual Arts, P.O. Box 18117, Minneapolis, MN 55418-0117 (the major national organization for Christians in the arts; publishes newsletter with openings and competitions for Christian artists and a directory of Christian artists, and sponsors biennial national conference; Sandra Bowden, president).

subject index

scripture index

William A. Dyrness (D.Théol., University of Strasbourg; Doctorandus, Free University) has been professor of theology and culture at Fuller Theological Seminary since 1990. He is a member of the board of advisers for the "Theology through the Arts" project formerly at Cambridge University, now at St. Andrews University, and a founding member of the Brehm Center for Theology, Worship, and the Arts, based at Fuller. The author of many books, including *The Earth Is God's: A Theology of American Culture* and *How Does America Hear the Gospel?* he is an ordained minister in the Presbyterian Church of the United States of America, husband of Grace, and father of three children.